You'll Never Know God Is All You Need Until You Realize God Is All You Have

Lamont McLaurin

Copyright ©2014 Lamont McLaurin

Publishing Consultant Diva Enterprise Books

All rights reserved.

ISBN-10: 0989393127
ISBN-13: 978-0989393126

FOREWORD

I am an avid reader of books of all genres and I have explored scores of books in my lifetime but none have compared to this manuscript where it actually gave a promise on the back of the book and actually delivered. As promised by the time I read from chapters 1-10 my life miraculously changed. Not only is "You Never Know" a page turner, but a human interest phenomenon, it actually answers and gives meaning to life's hard questions that people of all walks of life ponder daily. At the time of reading this book my life was at a standstill for approximately 3 years and I saw no way out, after completing this manuscript not only do I have balance in every area of my life but now I experience what I didn't experience before and that is success: not only spiritually, but socially, financially, mentally, physically, and relationally. The Purpose Driven Life by Rick Warren caused me to think. You Never Know caused me to prosper.

Todd King
Entrepreneur

You'll Never Know God Is All You Need Until You Realize God is All You Have

CONTENTS

1	If You Look For Me With All Your Heart, You Will Find Me	1
2	Does Calling on God Now Make Me A Hypocrite?	4
3	You Knew I Was A Snake When You Picked Me Up (Backsliding-the Condition of Man)	8
4	Why Does God Allow Bad Things to Happen to Good People?	12
5	One Day You're Drinking the Wine, the Next Day You're Stomping on the Grapes	14
6	Who is God?	19
7	Do All Religions Lead to God?	26
8	How Do I Find God?	32
9	What's So Special About That Jewish Carpenter?	39
10	Don't Trip!	43
11	God Don't Have No Partners	48
12	The Proof is in the Pudding	52
13	How Do I Pray Effectively?	55
14	How Can I Be Certain God is Answering My Prayers?	62
15	Can God Turn My Tragedy into Triumph?	65
16	If God Could Answer the Devil's Prayer I Know He'll Answer Mine	68
17	Go Thy Way, As Thou Has Believed	70
18	Cut Me In or Cut It Out	72
19	That One Mysterious Scripture	77
20	But By My Spirit	81

21	Dead and Stinking	85
22	You Have What You Say	89
23	It Must Be a Pony in There Somewhere	92
24	When I See the Blood	96
25	Silver and Gold I Do Not Have	99
26	When Chronos Meets Kairos	101
27	What You Walk Away From	107
28	One Hand Washes the Other, and Both Wash the Face	113
29	It Ain't Dat Deep	117
30	Don't Think it Strange	123
31	The Hickey Doo	130
32	Lord I Believe, but Help My Unbelief	135
33	Faith to Kill For	139
34	Running While Yet Still Dark	145
35	Inanimate Objects	148
36	What About Me?	153
37	Where Do We Go From Here?	163
38	You Can't Stop Me, You Can Only Hope to Contain Me	166
39	Can I Trust the Bible?	168
40	Did You Hear About Lamont?	176

1
IF YOU LOOK FOR ME WITH ALL YOUR HEART YOU WILL FIND ME

"Now a certain woman had a flow of blood for twelve years and suffered many things from many physicians. She had spent all that she had and was no better, but grew worse."

"She heard about Jesus…she came behind him in a crowd and touched the hem of His garment."

For she said, "If only I may touch His clothes, I shall be made well."

Immediately, the fountain of her blood dried up, and she felt in her body she was healed of her afflictions."

Mark 5:25-29

This is a true story. Its significance is - *in the same manner that God was the woman's last resort then, He is our last resort now!*

I believe this woman was rich or financially stable. Back in those days they didn't have Health Partners or medical subsidies; they had to pay with cold, hard cash. After she trusted money and logic had failed, she began to look for God. *At the end of logic and material assets you will always find the beginning of GOD.*

After this woman went broke, had no social life and was friendless she said in her heart "Let me look for God."

When you look for God, there is only one way to find Him and that is through "faith." In Hebrews 11:6 it says:

"For it is impossible to please God without Faith, You must first believe that He is and He is a rewarder of those who diligently seek Him."

This woman, pressing through crowds of thousands, demonstrated to Christ *she believed*. By healing her, *Jesus demonstrated that her* faith made her whole. It is crucial that when you look for God, you do not seek Him through philosophy, human intellect or the like, but with your heart.

When a person is diagnosed with cancer, AIDS, kidney failure, or experiences such as foreclosure, evictions, etc., he or she will believe anything that God reveals, because *tribulation preps you to be introduced to God.*

Prior to tribulation you believe what you want to believe about God (a whole host of notions):

- A statue is God
- The sun is God
- The moon is God
- Jesus is not the son of God
- The Bible is tampered with

What happens when things go wrong, like?

- The judge says "I sentence you to thirty years,".... "OH GOD!"
- The doctor says, "Mr. Johnson, we have done all we can do,." "OH GOD!"
- When you come from work and the orange sign on your door says "Sheriff's Sale,." "OH GOD!"

Then your heart is ripe for God's entrance. Things that you laughed about pre-tribulation you speak about with conviction - post tribulation.

It's a heart matter and when you look for God with all your heart you will find Him

2
DOES CALLING ON GOD MAKE ME A HYPOCRITE

When a man is first born, he is absent of the knowledge of God. Romans 3:10-11: *As it is written: there is none righteous, no not one. There is none who understands, there is none who seeks God.* When God describes a "hypocrite" in the Bible, he talks of people who claim to know Him, but live their lives the exact opposite of what they confess they believe. All religions have them, but none have them more than the Christian faith!

On the front cover of this book, you see four different people, of varying nationalities from different vocations (with different issues). There are two things that link them all together:

- They are all experiencing tribulation.

- Their tribulation caused them all to seek God.

Let's examine my theory, in light of these four personalities (on the front cover of this manuscript):

Michael Vick

Michael Vick is clearly one of the most colorful, entertaining football players who ever played the game. I am a great fan of his. I watched him when he first came to the league and when he contracted with the Atlanta Falcons He received a multi-million dollar contract, to the tune of $130 Million. He thanked everyone but one person... God! What was telling was when he received an indictment for illegal dog fighting, he never mentioned God! But when he found that his friends were cooperating against him during a public interview, he showed contrition for his actions and made this amazing statement: *I thank my Lord & savior Jesus Christ...*

Is he a hypocrite?

Hugo Chavez:

Chavez is the president of Venezuela, who spent much of his time supporting the socialist ideas of famed Atheist Karl Marx and Fidel Castro. When diagnosed with cancer, he was observed carrying a picture of Jesus Christ during his caravan from Mira Flores Presidential Palace.

Is this hypocrisy?

Paris Whitney Hilton:

Paris is an American heiress of the Hilton fortune, socialite, television personality and businesswoman. My personal observation of her is that she leads a purely secular lifestyle. At the time of her latest bout with the law, she was spotted going to court with a gold Bible. Never before in public did she mention the word God.

Would you say this diva, heiress of millions, social butterfly is a hypocrite?

The Family from Sandy Hook:

(I don't know these people personally, so I can only guesstimate here)

This family could have awakened that morning, ate breakfast together and planned a family outing for later that evening. When they heard the tragic news of their loved ones demise, they went to the scene and began to call on God.

Were they hypocrites for calling on God during the crisis?

World Trade Center Attacks (911)
America the greatest nation on the planet earth - blessed by God with her exotic liberties, blessed institutions and superior military might – fell to her knees on September 11, 2001.

- Did she fall because her educational system improved?
- Did her economy hit an all-time high?
- Did she find the cure for cancer?

None of the above! On September 11, 2001 America experienced the worst terrorist attack right on her soil! I physically witnessed this being just sixteen blocks away. *(*Please see Did You Hear about Lamont?)* People I observed daily – doctors, lawyers, hospital workers, etc., started racing down the street as if they were in a Bull Run...bleeding, bruised, with broken limbs screaming one of two things:

1. God help us!
2. Jesus, help me

Are they hypocrites? Absolutely not! They are just people who came to the stark reality that you will never know God is all you need, until you realize God is all you have! Let's face it, when cops and firefighters are dying, who do you call?

Approximately two years ago a student posed a very good question that most humans ponder daily. He asked, "Hey Lamont, why do people only run to God when they have troubles?" His question took me to the Bible in Matthew 24:1, 21, with special emphasis on verse 21:

The disciples were sitting on the Mt. of Olives questioning Jesus about the end times; as Jesus prophesied about earthquakes, false prophets, wars and the destruction of the Temple (all of which have come true) He then gave this startling prophecy *...and there will be tribulation in this world like never seen before, and never to be seen* *again.*

You might ask the question, "Why Tribulation God?"
King David, a biblical character, and a man after God's own heart, gave the answer to this mystery over 3,000 years ago when he uttered these words by the inspiration of the Holy Ghost, in Psalms 119:67: *Before I was afflicted I went astray...*

Tribulation is a soul converter. Most people get soul and spirit confused, but they are mutually exclusive properties. Your soul encompasses your will, emotions, desires and intellect. Your spirit is where your conscience is housed. When your soul is afflicted it turns to its manufacturer, God!

Genesis 2:8
God breathed the breath of life and man began to be a living soul.

So when the people above began to pray and call on God they came to the realization that no other alternative existed to stop the affliction of their soul; they turned to the creator of their souls, God! God doesn't look at humans as hypocrites. To put it another way, He looks at our afflictions as a perfect opportunity to come into an intimate relationship with us, the crowing jewels of his creation.

Come to me all who are heavy laden and burdened and I will give you rest for your souls. *(*Matthew 11:28)

3
YOU KNEW I WAS A SNAKE WHEN YOU PICKED ME UP
(BACKSLIDING-THE CONDITION OF MAN)

A hunter went out to hunt for snakes and stumbled across a snake that was already wounded. As he approached the snake, he had compassion and felt compelled to help it. As the story plays out, the hunter changed his mind, pointed his shotgun at the snake and just as he prepared to kill him; the snake uttered "Please don't kill me, please don't kill me! Just let me lay here and die." At that point the hunter picked up the snake, took him to the nearest veterinarian then took him home to keep as a pet and nursed him back to health. The snake ate dinner at the family table, had its own special quarters, went on trips with the family, etc. One day the hunter stuck his hand in the cage to feed the snake and the snake lashed out and bit him. As the venom attacked his immune system, he slowly passed out.

Before the hunter died, he questioned the snake for the reason for its betrayal:

"I found you dying in the woods, was prepared to shoot you and sell your skin for money. Instead, I took you to the vet and spent a great deal of money to get you healed. I took you home, made you a part of my family, you ate at our dinner table, went on family trips, celebrated holidays. Why, why, why, why would you bite me knowing that your bite would kill me?"

The snake responded "You knew I was a snake when you picked me up!"

Often-times you hear this little voice that says "God won't accept you; he won't answer your prayers, and you are a hypocrite. He won't forgive you. Why don't you continue in rebellion and disobedience?" It is not the voice of God! It's the voice of Satan! As sure as God is real, the devil is as real as the skin on your hand!

God has spoken to man through His word telling him, "I know who you are, and that is why I prepared the twins Grace and Mercy."

God says something very important in these specific chapters:
- Jeremiah 17:9-10

The heart is deceitful above all things, and desperately wicked: who can know it? (9)

I the LORD search the heart, I try the reins, even to give every man according to his ways, and according to the fruit of his doings (10)

- Psalms 103:13-14

Like as a father pitieth his children, so the LORD pitieth them that fear him.
For he knoweth our frame; he remembereth that we are dust.

- Romans 7:15, 18, 19

For that which I do I allow not: for what I would, that do I not; but what I hate, that do I. (15)
For I know that in me (that is, in my flesh,) dwelleth no good thing: for to will is present with me; but how to perform that which is good I find not. (18)
For the good that I would I do not: but the evil which I would not, that I do. (19)

In Jeremiah, God tells us that the condition of our heart is desperately wicked, so wicked that nobody could know how wicked it is. The heart refers to the mind the source of thinking, feeling and action.

In Psalms 103, God tells us that He feels sorry for people who worship Him because he remembers that our frame is from the dust. What is God communicating?

When Adam sinned, the earth's ground was cursed. We derived from the ground from the dust, so when God says he remembers our frame is from the dust He is saying that He remembers that we are cursed people, inherited from our forefather Adam. Remember all things are made after their own kind. *What is the curse and why are we cursed?* The curse is found in Romans 7:15.18-19:

You see the Apostle Paul, a man converted from Judaism to Christianity, (who was brought to an end of himself) stated that the good that he promised God he didn't do, but the sin he promised God he wouldn't do - he practiced. Wow! Raise your hand if that is a portrait of you.

I am an educator at a Christian School. During devotions, the teachers were complaining about the students not getting to class on time. So one day we played a prank on the students. We staged a fake brawl between four students. All through the hallway you could hear "Fight, fight, fight!" As the kids were running with breakneck speed to my classroom, I said 'I told you I would get you in here on time.'

Why were the students on time? Because cursed things are more appealing than blessed things to a human being. That is why God gave us the gift of the Holy Spirit to lift the curse off of us. The Bible says ...*and we know that the entire world is under the sway (influence) of the devil. For this reason we must be born again.*

In the Book of II Samuel 11:1-27, there is a story about a king that Almighty God said was a man after His own heart. His name was King David. What puzzles me is how God could say that this man was anything to Him after what he did. King David not only had sex with his best friend's wife while he was at war; he got her pregnant. When David couldn't blame the pregnancy on his best friend, he sent the general of his army a note to put his best friend at the front of the battle so he could be executed; that is what happened! So how could God call an apparent low-life a man after

His heart? The answer is in Psalms 51:1-6 in chronological order:

1. He asked to be forgiven according to who God is. (A God of Mercy)
2. He asked to be thoroughly cleansed. Not that he would clean himself. (Dependency on God)
3. He's saying he knew exactly what he did and because there is a curse on his flesh it could happen again.
4. He acknowledges that although his friend suffered the offence, God ultimately suffered also.
5. Again he recognizes his condition, a born sinner. Born to do wrong against God.
6. He's telling God that he knows what God expects.

When you acknowledge your condition and feel sorry in your heart that's when change comes. Have you ever wondered why Adam never found favor with God? The reason is because when Adam backslid he lied about it, he attempted to cover it. He blamed it on Eve, the snake, and lastly God. He never knew his condition. So it's not the fact that you backslide, it's how you are going to slide back that matters most with God.

4
WHY DOES GOD ALLOW BAD THINGS TO HAPPEN TO GOOD PEOPLE

First, to ask the question is to confuse categories. *The proper question to ask is "Why does God permit more good than evil?"*

If you do a census on this country alone, if we have a population of 300 million, how many are in prisons? - Probably less than 3%. If God was a God that permits or encourages evil, then that statistic would probably go up to 90-95%

You may then ask "Well, didn't God create good and evil?" The answer is No! He created a potential for evil.

Example #1:
When a prison administrator gives an inmate a comb and a toothbrush, what is the specific intent for the comb and toothbrush? The comb is to groom one's hair and the toothbrush is to clean one's teeth; both are actions you have to agree are good. But if an inmate gets angry at another inmate and decides to make a shank (a homemade knife) out of the comb and toothbrush and commit homicide with them, is it the prison official's fault, God's fault or the prisoner's fault? *If you are committed to truth, you will answer that it is the prisoner's fault or the human heart.*

First you must acknowledge that God created the potential for evil because God created human beings with freedom of choice to love, hate, do good or evil. Furthermore, without choice, love is meaningless. God is neither a cosmic rapist who forces his love on people nor a puppeteer who forces people to love Him. Instead, God is the personification of love, grants us the freedom of choice, and the record of history bears eloquent testimony to the fact that humans of their own free will have actualized the reality of evil through choice.

Example #2:
Lay down 100 machines guns in the middle of Bronx, NY and seal it off so humans can't come inside the gates. Not one act of violence will be perpetrated, but open the gates and allow humans to come in and watch the chaos. Is it God perpetrating the violence or the human heart? Answer: it's the human heart. God is innocent!

Matthew 15:19:
For out of the human heart proceeds evil thoughts, murders, adulteries, fornications, thefts, lies and blasphemies.

Question: Does God have a purpose for evil?
Answer: Yes.

God takes evil circumstances and turns them around for good (Romans 8:28); that's what makes God a sovereign God.
And we know that all things work together for good to them that love God, to them who are the called according to his purpose.(Romans8:28)

5
ONE DAY YOU'RE DRINKING THE WINE, THE NEXT DAY YOU'RE STOMPING THE GRAPES

Before you can experience God, you must come to an end of yourself.

As Jesus said in His Olivet discourse *"blessed are those who are poor in spirit."* What does it mean to be poor in spirit? It means to wholly depend on the one who created you. It means to trust the Lord thy God with all your heart and not to lean on your own understanding and to acknowledge Him in all your ways. In short, check your pride at the door. The battle is not yours, it's the Lord's.

There is an all familiar story in the Book of Exodus and Genesis that coined the term "God pimped the devil". It is in Genesis 15:13, where God predicts that the Jews would go into slavery for 400 years and that he would raise a deliverer (Moses) among them to bring them out. Like clockwork, one thousand years later it happens. The Jews are in slavery in Egypt.

Pharaoh obviously overheard one of the Jews talking about a deliverer coming because the 400 years was coming to fruition. Pharaoh, your type of "devil," came up with this ingenious plan: to kill all of the firstborn and the deliverer would never come. Well, to make a long story short, Almighty God, the Master Planner and Supreme Genius, put Pharaoh's plan to an abysmal shame.

First, God stirred His spirit among the nurses or midwives to obey Him not Pharaoh. So when Moses was born, they put him in the river. Where did God direct Moses? He floated straight to Pharaoh's daughter. Who was asked to fetch the Pharaoh's daughter a nurse for her? Moses' sister, Miriam. Who did Miriam get? Moses' mother Yoshabell. Did Yoshabell raise Moses? Yes. Who paid Yoshabell? Pharaoh's daughter.

So as the rest of the story goes God raised His deliverer in Pharaohs' own house, and Pharaoh paid for it.

What was in Pharaohs' house?

1. Power
2. Women
3. Money
4. Friends
5. Authority
6. Education

Why couldn't God use Moses in that capacity?

Moses had to come to an end of himself, like you and I must. Then he could become relational with God. When did Moses become relational with God? Was it when:

1. He had power and authority in Pharaohs' house?
2. When he was the most popular person in Egypt?
3. When all the women flocked to him?

No, it was when Moses killed the Egyptian, and it was discovered. Did he find God?

Question: Where did Moses find God?

Answer: In a burning bush in the desert.

Question: Why do you think God showed Himself to Moses in a burning bush in the desert at that time?

Answer: I believe God was in that burning bush the entire time, and I believe Moses traveled that route 100's of times, but before Moses couldn't recognize God. He had to be humbled when he no longer had:
1. women
2. power
3. popularity
4. money

Hello...God! Moses was brought to an end of himself in the desert, and that's where God speaks to us best in our "desert place." How many times has God attempted to talk to you through prosperity? We can't hear Him, but when all hell breaks loose we seem to hear Him loud and clear. Moses heard Him and was not only delivered, but ordained "The Deliverer."

When a man comes to the end of himself, he sees things from God's perspective and not from mans' limited point of view..

I want to share a story with you about two men from Iraq. Both wielded great power and might. I believe both men (I am certain of one) looked for God. They found Him, came to their end, and were saved. These two men were Nebuchadnezzar and Saddam Hussein. Nebuchadnezzar was a 2700 B.C. king in Babylon that is presently the modern day Iraq that President Saddam Hussein patterned himself after. He coined himself the modern-day Nebuchadnezzar. Not only figuratively but literally, because on Iraqi currency there was a picture of Nebuchadnezzar on one side and Saddam on the other. It is utterly amazing how Bible prophecy connects the two.

King Nebuchadnezzar was a very powerful king that God had elevated, who didn't honor Him as God, but worshipped idols and himself. He was troubled by terrible dreams that none of his astrologers or soothsayers could interpret. He summoned Daniel a young Hebrew man whom the Spirit of the living God was in. Daniel interpreted his dreams. Through interpretation he told the king that if he did not pursue righteousness, break off his sins, and show mercy that Almighty God would drive him from the face of men. His dwelling would be with the beast of the field and he would eat grass like oxen. He gave the counsel some thought for about a year, turned, and disrespected the word that was sent from Almighty God.

His response: *'Is this not great Babylon that I have built for the house of the Kingdom by the might of my power and for the majesty of my honor.'*

While the words were still in his mouth, a voice was heard from heaven saying: *O' King Nebuchadnezzar, to you it is spoken, your kingdom has departed. And they shall drive thee from men and your dwelling shall be with the beast of the field, you shall eat grass like oxen until you know that the most high rules in the Kingdom of men.* In that same hour, it was fulfilled. He was driven from men; he ate grass, his body was wet with the dew from heaven, his hair grew like eagle's feathers and his nails like bird's claws.

At the end of his days, he lifted his eyes to heaven and his understanding returned to him. He blessed the Most High God, praised and exalted him. You see, this man had to become insane and animal like in his habits and senses to come to the end of himself.

In that condition, he would learn more about God than he ever would. The purpose of the judgment was so he could know who the true and living God was. He had to be humbled before he was exalted. Once he was humbled, he unmistakably acknowledged Daniel's God as the Sovereign God.

What's telling is Saddam Hussein had a very similar end. Several nations wanted Saddam because of the poor treatment of his people. He ignored everyone. Then the U.S. and a coalition of nations came and killed his sons and took his kingdom. When he was captured (pay close attention to this) he was found on a farm, in a hole covered with grass; his hair looked like eagles feathers. He was holding a picture of Jesus. Saddam was a Muslim. Why was he in his last days of tribulation holding a picture of Jesus? Things that make you say hmmmmmm!

Like Moses and Nebuchadnezzar, we must always come to an end of ourselves. This is probably the reason why today we often stay in prolonged states of tribulation. You may think God has forgotten about you, but He hasn't. He just wants you to stop trying to fix it, stop leaning on your own limited understanding and trust His infinite understanding. Stand still and know that He is God alone!

Our unknown future is secure in the hands of an all knowing GOD!

6
WHO IS GOD

In order for something to be "God," the most ardent skeptic would have to agree,
God must possess these three attributes:

1. He must be Omnipotent. Omnipotence is an exclusive attribute of God, and it is essential to the perfection of His being. In order to be God, he must have power over everything that has power over you and all things created.

2. He must be Omnipresent. Omnipresence is also an exclusive attribute of God free from laws that limit Him in time or space. Although God is distinct from all His works, His power, intelligence and goodness penetrate them all. So in the dynamic sense, God is everywhere at all times.

3. He must have perfect knowledge. The knowledge must relate to Him and anything beyond Himself. If He didn't know all things then you couldn't put faith and trust in Him. If you couldn't trust Him, He would be disqualified as God.

The only faith that possesses these essential attributes is Christianity. How could I say such a thing? Let's take a look at world religions versus Christianity:

- Islam
- Buddhism
- Hinduism

In Christianity God reveals Himself through His spoken word! Underscored below are the three attributes that proves His deity.

<u>Omnipotence:</u>
- Gen 17:1:

And when Abram was ninety years old and nine, the LORD appeared to Abram, and said unto him, I am the Almighty God; walk before me, and be thou perfect.

- Deuteronomy 3:24:

O Lord GOD, thou hast begun to shew thy servant thy greatness, and thy mighty hand: for what God is there in heaven or in earth, that can do according to thy works, and according to thy might?

<u>Omnipresence:</u>
- Psalms 139:7, 8:

Whither shall I go from thy spirit? or whither shall I flee from thy presence? If I ascend up into heaven, thou art there: if I make my bed in hell, behold, thou art there.

- Jeremiah 23:23, 24:

Am I a God at hand, saith the LORD, and not a God afar off? Can any hide himself in secret places that I shall not see him? saith the LORD. Do not I fill heaven and earth? saith the LORD.

Omniscience:
- Psalms 33:13, 14

The LORD looketh from heaven; he beholdeth all the sons of men. (13) From the place of his habitation he looketh upon all the inhabitants of the earth. (14)

- Hebrew 4:13

Neither is there any creature that is not manifest in his sight: but all things are naked and opened unto the eyes of him with whom we have to do. (13)

BUDDHISM

Let's first deal with one of the fastest growing religions on the face of the earth. Its creator was a prince who made himself a pauper named Siddhartha Gautama who was proclaimed to be the first psychologist. Nevertheless, he was agnostic. He was skeptical that God existed. A logical corollary suggests that if a religion is skeptical of God then that the religion does not believe in the attributes of God. So while Buddhism claims to give you enlightenment, it only enlightens as far as the frail mind can. It is not all knowing, all powerful, and ever present.

So I pose this question:

- Is the Buddhist's deity God?

ISLAM

In Islam, there are great philosophies and similarities to Christianity such as belief in the virgin birth, a sinless Christ and return of Christ but it fails the acid test in omniscience.

In Surat 53:19 the great prophet Muhammad asks a very disturbing question to his Arab contemporaries in Mecca that rejected Islam: *Have you considered Allat, Manat, Sua and Uzza. These were other deities that the Arabs worshipped in the Kaba.* The apology was that the great prophet had mistakenly heard from Satan.

I respectfully have two problems with that theology:

1. The first problem is when the great prophet uttered the statement, whether from God or Satan. It shows indecisiveness which shows lack of omniscience.

2. Secondly, if the apology or reasoning is true and the great prophet did hear from Satan. When did Satan start speaking to him and when did Satan stop. Because that question cannot be rationally answered I place this question in your lap:

- Is Islam's god God?

HINDUISM

Hinduism is a religion that believes in hundreds of god's and because out of the many gods' none share the same attributes collectively. This respectfully and theologically disqualifies Hinduism as having the true omnipotent omniscient, omnipresent God.

Here's a great question I would like to ask:

- Are the many gods of Hinduism the *True and Living God?*

WHY DID JESUS SAY HE WAS GOD?

While I verify this, I might as well multitask and answer the question, "Does the Bible say that Jesus is God?"

Did Jesus Say He was God?

Like the Trinity, the incarnation is often considered to be logically incoherent. While it may transcend our human understanding, it does not transgress the laws of logic. Because God created humanity in His own image, the essential properties of human nature (rationale, will, moral character, emotions, etc.) is not inconsistent with His divine nature. Though the notion of God becoming an oyster would be absurd, the reality that God became a man is not. The natural man recoils at the notion of God becoming a man and has intractable difficulties believing the theory that Jesus was one person with two different distinct natures, 100% man and 100% God.

Let's deal with the first question.

When Jesus came to Caesarea Philippi, He asked this very profound question: *Who do men say that I am?*

Mormons answer this question by saying that Jesus is the spirit brother of Lucifer. Jehovah Witnesses answer this question by saying He is the Arch Angel Michael. New Agers say Jesus is an Avatar or an enlightened messenger. Jesus however, answered by claiming He was God (Revelations 1:8). Below are a few supporting scriptures: that a blind person couldn't miss the import.

John 14:7-9

In this text, Jesus is having a discussion with His disciples who were all Jews and believed in one God. In the most literal sense, He says to Phillip, *If you had known me you would have known my Father or God and from this point not only do you know Him but you see Him.*

John 8:53-58

Jesus is having a very intense discussion about His identity with the Jews. At the end of the discussion, He used terminology that was an exclusive prerogative only for God when He said *Before Abraham was I AM.* Associating yourself with "I AM" was the height of blasphemy. Why? Because when Moses asked God His name in Exodus 3:13, 14, God responds saying His name was *I AM.*

Revelation 1:8 states, *I am Alpha and Omega, the beginning and the ending, saith the Lord, which is, which was, and which is to come, the Almighty.*

When Jesus referred to Himself as the *Alpha and the Omega, the first and the last*, it's overwhelmingly clear that He is referring to the same name as the Jehovah of the Old Testament in Isaiah 41:4 and He leaves no middle ground for conjecture.

What do I mean by "conjecture?" Well, if you read the gospel, Jesus is referred to as a Prophet, Son of God and God, which all were His offices.

There are verses that leave a person wondering if He is God, such as John 10:29 where *He says My Father is greater than I.* The meaning of that verse is referring to Jesus' dual nature. Christ was referring to rank not deity. God the Father is 100% God, not 100% man and 100% God. Therefore, Jesus was drawing a distinction, not suggesting that He was not fully God.

Finally, Jesus claimed to possess the very same attributes of God.

- He claimed omniscience when He predicted the fall of the temple in Matthew 24:1.
- He declared omnipotence by not only resurrecting Lazarus from the dead in John 11:43, but raising Himself from the dead in John 2:19
- He professed omnipresence by promising the disciples that He would be with them always until the end of the age (Matthew 28:20). Not only that, Jesus said to the paralytic in Luke 5:20: *Friend your sins are forgiven.* In doing so, He claimed an exclusive prerogative of God alone.
- If that's not enough, in the Koran, Muhammad pronounced Jesus sinless in Surat 19:17. Sinless out of the entire human race demonstrates that He was not just a good moral teacher, or nice Prophet, but declared and determined to be God.

Now does the Bible claim that Jesus was God? The answer: Absolutely!

There are scores of biblical text that is not only clear but convincing that states that Jesus is God:

1. John 1:1
In the beginning was the Word, and the Word was with God and the Word was God. Here Jesus is not only in existence before the world began but is differentiated from the Father and explicitly called God, indicating that He shares the same nature as the Father.

2. Colossians 1:16
...All things were created by Him; verse 17: *He is before all things,* verse 19: *...and God was pleased to have all His fullness dwell in him.* Only deity has authority over creation, pre-exists all things and has the full nature of God.

3. Hebrews 1: 8-9
Clearly tells us that according to God the Father Himself, Jesus is God; but about the Son He, (the Father says) *Your throne, O' God, will last forever and ever.* It stretches credulity to the breaking point to clearly miss what the Bible says about Christ. Last but not least in

my opinion, this verse left me awe struck with respect to what the Bible says about the deity of Christ.

   4. I Corinthians 10:1-4

The writer of this verse was a Jew who abhorred and murdered Christians. But through divine intervention and revelation the Apostle Paul transcribed it. When you read the verse you will see that Paul is speaking to a Jewish audience about the exodus experience where God appeared to them in a cloud and fed them spiritually from a rock, and Paul shockingly says that Rock was Christ. How could the Rock be Christ when Christ is at least 1600 years separated from the Exodus event? The answer is simple. What Paul is attempting to say is the God of the Old Testament and Christ are the same.

7
DO ALL RELIGIONS LEAD TO GOD

Recently, while writing this chapter, I experienced a very strange phenomenon. I received a text from an Elder of the church I attend, notifying me that a gentleman from our Thursday night Bible study was murdered. When I asked what happened, he said all he knew was it was over an argument about religion.

Simultaneously, while receiving the shocking news, a young man arrived at the institution where I was working looking quite disheveled. While processing his intake report, he shared with me the fact that he just witnessed a murder. I asked what happened. He said it was two guys arguing over religion. It was the same incident. At the conclusion of the conversation the young man said "It's a shame one man is dead, and another lost his freedom all over a silly argument about religion. Don't all religions lead to God anyway?"

This may be one of the most frequent questions asked in theology, and the answer is NO! God never made religion. He made relationship. I know it's an awfully bold statement so I will prove my case!

Okay. First, when you begin to examine world religions such as Judaism, Hinduism and Buddhism, you will immediately recognize that all the religions directly contradict one another. For example, Moses taught that there was ONE God. Krishna believed in hundreds of Gods, and Buddha was a skeptic. Now logically they can all be wrong, but it is impossible for them to all be right.

Now if we need a bit more dispelling of the theory lets test this simple but powerful example:

To say that all religions lead to God is to say that all views are equally valid. If indeed all views are equally valid, then the Christian view must be equally valid, which holds that not all views are equally valid.

For instance:

Acts 4:12:
Neither is there salvation in any other: for there is none other name under heaven given among men, whereby we must be saved.

John 14:6:
Jesus saith unto him, I am the way, the truth, and the life: no man cometh unto the Father, but by me.

So, the Christian view says that the only way to heaven is through Jesus Christ, and humans say all religions lead to God. Then if all religions are the correct way, then when the Bible says "No man comes to God but through Jesus – we must assume that is correct.

(Now that we have concluded through logical deduction that not all religions lead to God, we now have to establish God's original intent for mankind. To understand the past and future of mankind and to appreciate the present state of men's journey through time, it is crucial to consider God's original purpose and plan for creation.)

If you study the Bible, the word kingdom appears at least 200 times, 85% percent of the time in the New Testament. What was

Jesus communicating to mankind? The original intent of the establishment of God's original kingdom was to establish a kingdom of kings to extend His ruler-ship, will and nature from heaven to earth. His desire was to manifest His glorious character, wisdom, righteous judgments and purposes in the earth realm through the administrative leadership of mankind on earth. The ultimate goal of God the Creator was to colonize earth with heaven and establish it as a visible territory of an invisible world. His purpose was to establish a heavenly kingdom on earth just as things are in heaven.

God's purpose in the beginning was to:

1) Establish a family of spirit sons, not servants
2) Establish a kingdom, not a religious organization
3) Establish a kingdom of kings, not subjects
4) Establish a commonwealth of citizens not religious members
5) Extend His heavenly government to earth and influence earth from heaven through mankind.

The Loss of the Kingdom (Miles Monroe)

To understand the loss of the Adamic kingdom mandate, it is important to realize you cannot lose what you never had. Adam, the first royal representative of heaven's earthly kingdom on earth, was delegated the responsibility of serving as heaven's earthly ambassador.

An ambassador is only as viable and legal as his relationship with his Government. Therefore, the most important relationship Adam had on earth was with heaven. This is why the Holy Spirit of God was intimate with mankind from the very beginning. His indwelling presence guaranteed constant communication and fellowship with the will, mind, intent and purposes of God and heaven so he could execute His government's will on earth. This relationship made the Holy Spirit of God the most important person on earth and established Him as the Key component of the Kingdom of Heaven and earth. The loss or separation of man from the Holy Spirit of God would render mankind a disqualified envoy of heaven and earth, for through the separation he would not know the will or mind of the government of Heaven and earth.

However, God had a significant response to this defection and egregious act of treason. It is recorded in Genesis 3:15-16:

And I will put enmity between you and the woman, and between your offspring and hers, He will crush our head, and you will strike his heel.

The heart of this promise is the coming of an offspring through a virgin woman who would break the power of the adversary over mankind and regain the authority and dominion Adam once held, and through a process called salvation, restore the Kingdom back to mankind. Therefore, the greatest need of men was identified by what he lost; he did not lose a religion or heaven. He lost a kingdom.

Religion, therefore, is a man's futile attempt to search for God. No matter how dedicated, zealous, loyal, or faithful he is to his religious pursuit, it is tantamount to chasing a ghost if a man hasn't found the kingdom. No matter if you are Buddhist, Muslim, Hindu, Judaism, etc.

Well, what about Christians? Christianity is a faith, not a religion. Nowhere in the Bible did God call believers Christians. He called us sons, daughters, servants, saints not Christians. The name appears in the Bible only three times: Acts 11:26 Acts 26:28-29, 1 Peter 4:16-17.

Please do not be offended by the fact the word "Christian" has too much baggage attached to it and most of it has nothing to do with the kingdom of God.

We were first called Christians because people observed our "Christ-likeness," lifestyle, power and boldness. In essence, Christianity was supposed to be the culture of the kingdom demonstrated through our lives - demonstrating a relationship with God, not religion.

Last but not least let's discuss the subject of sin:

Approximately a year ago, a young lady asked me a question in a Theology class I was instructing. The atmosphere was somewhat noisy the day when she asked the question. You could not hear a pin drop. "Hey brother Lamont, my mommy is a Christian and my daddy is a Muslim. Who's going to hell and who is going to heaven? Well, I disguised my nervousness. I then bowed my head, went into a quick meditation with God's Holy Spirit and boy did God give a righteous revelatory answer.

I told the class to turn to John chapter 4:1-29. It is the story about the Samaritan woman at the well. When Jesus encountered this woman He didn't go into a dissertation about Judaism or even discuss religion with her. She attempted to debate with Christ, Jesus simply asked for a drink of water and exposed her sin and she ran back to her city and told people that Jesus was in fact God. I then queried the class:

1. If a man murdered another man and he was found guilty at trial and at sentencing, the judge gave the man probation what type of judge would he be?

Response: "A cool judge!"

Since they were not committed to truth, I redirected more questions:

2. "What if that man was your dad?"

Response: "A bad judge."

3. "Is God a judge?"

Response: A resounding, "YES!"

4. "Would God be a bad judge if he didn't punish sin?"

Amazingly they responded, "Yes."

Then I wrote on the chalkboard:

"It's not your parent's religion that is the question; the question is who pays for their sin?"

The young lady tearfully dropped her head and said, "Jesus!" The class began to applaud, Muslims and Christians; because instead of this big theological debate about religion leaving someone wounded, they received a spiritual answer that left their hearts healed.

8
HOW DO I FIND GOD?

In every man's life, there must be an authority that is definitive (no middle ground, I mean absolute!) I cannot think of anything on this earth that should be more definite than the Almighty God! Titles like "creator," "supreme being" and "god of my understanding" only demonstrate that you are not sure who God is. Eternally speaking, it's really a travesty to be in that position.

Almighty God said to the prophet Jeremiah (while the children of Israel were in slavery in Babylon), *If you seek ME with all your heart you will find ME.* The effectual words are *"seek"* and *"heart."* You see when you seek God with your whole heart you reveal your true character to God, and then God reveals Himself to you through His true character.

And ye shall seek me, and find me, when ye shall search for me with all your heart. (Jeremiah 29:13)

With all your heart means a heart with honest, pure intentions.

God said in the Book of Jeremiah:

The heart is deceitful above all things, and desperately wicked: who can know it? (Jeremiah 17:9)

Do you remember the initial Rodney King verdict? How could that jury come back with a verdict of not guilty? The facts were overwhelming. There was empirical evidence that the cops were guilty of brutality, yet the jury had insuperable difficulty rendering a guilty verdict. Let me state for the record - the truth of the matter was the cops were guilty as sin for brutalizing Rodney King. Why couldn't an honest, conservative, and upstanding jury do what was right? Because most of the cops on trial, if not all, grew up in Simi Valley and had social, ethnic, and political roots together. Because of these circumstances, a "Not Guilty" verdict was reached.

Did the jury reach the verdict with their intellect? The answer is no. They justified it collectively in their hearts. Although a traffic light may be green and all evidence says it's green, if I want to believe that it is red, then that light will be red to me. This reasoning is called "free will," and it's important to note that your will is located in your heart.

the mistake we make when seeking God, is when we look for Him through reasoning or our own intellect.. The Bible says, *every way in a man's mind is right to him.* Our mind is limited. God is eternal, so any way that we fathom "God" in our mind is false. The only two co-eternal beings and witnesses of God (in antiquity) who can speak of God are Jesus Christ and the Holy Spirit:

I have glorified thee on the earth: I have finished the work which thou gavest me to do.
And now, O Father, glorify thou me with thine own self with the glory which I had with thee before the world was. (John 17:4-5)

In the beginning God created the heaven and the earth. (1)
And the earth was without form, and void; and darkness was upon the face of the deep. And the Spirit of God moved upon the face of the waters. (2) (Genesis 1:1-2)

And God said, Let us make man in our image, after our likeness: and let them have dominion over the fish of the sea, and over the fowl of the air, and over the cattle, and over all the earth, and over every creeping thing that creepeth upon the earth.
(Genesis 1:26)

Once we establish who God is, then we must become familiar with His name. You might ask why His name is so important. We all know that He is the Supreme Being, but that is not sufficient. You see you cannot go to the manufacturer of Mercedes Benz and say "Hey you should save some money and use Hyundai labels on your cars." What's in a name? In a name are two things: character and glory. Place a Hyundai label on a Benz, and a buyer expects to pay a Hyundai price. It's the same with God. If you inappropriately define God, you can confine God. If you define Him with your limited mind, then you confine His miracles in your life. Jesus said in Mark 11:24, *Whatever things you ask believing when you pray you will receive them.* Well, if you are praying to a distant God that you have no personal relationship with and don't know His name, nature or character, I can't imagine you believing Him for much, or anything or even knowing what to ask for.

When God called Abram, a man who lived in Iraq and whose ancestors were idol worshippers, He first introduced himself and told Abram how he should conduct himself in a relationship with Him (Almighty God). God said that His name was "El Shaddai" the "Big Breasted One" which is translated the Lord Almighty. Why was it important for God to reveal His name to Abram? Because Abram was an idol worshipper and most of his idols had breasts which translated "strength;" he had a rain god, sun god, moon god, fertility god, etc.

What was God communicating to Abram? You see God knew that a dumb idol cannot, walk, talk, breathe, answer prayer, etc. God knew that Abram was tormented by the fact that he had no children in his advanced age and knew that the dumb idols could not perform what only He could perform, so He used the opportunity to show Himself as immense. When He introduced Himself as "El Shaddai," the "Big Breasted One," he essentially told Abram that all his idols have been useless and are useless. Everything he looked for in them is in Him. That must have blown Abram's mind.

As the story closes in Genesis Chapters 12 to 23, God made Abram rich, and gave him children when he was in his late nineties and was anatomically unable to produce children. Abram reciprocated by dedicating his life to God and telling people who God is, and what the benefits were for serving Him.

God has many names:

- Jehovah Shalom – God of Peace
- Jehovah Ropha – God that is a Healer
- Jehovah Rohi – The Lord A Shepherd
- Jehovah Jerih – The Lord that Provides
- Jehovah Shammah – The Lord of Righteous

Why so many names? The answer is because God will meet you in any situation like:

- The crack house
- The court house
- The hospital
- The shelter
- The unemployment line
- The club
- Your heartache
- Your loneliness
- Your handicap
- Real estate foreclosure
- In your shame
- In your divorce
- In your suicide contemplation
- In your grief

It's imperative that you identify with God through His name, because in His name is His being, His holiness, omniscience, might, and sovereignty. If we just used terms like "Supreme Being" or "God of my understanding," politically correct terms, God would not get His Glory and if He cannot be glorified, then why should He perform a miracle? It's like the Miami Heat and Baltimore Ravens winning the championship, and commissioners Stern and Goodell turn and give the OKC Thunder and San

Francisco 49ers the rings and trophies. Could you get production out of the champs? No! Why not? There's no motivation! It's the same with God. How is God going to get His glory? When you call on Him by the proper use of His name He then can grant a miracle.

Approximately 2900 years ago there was a prophet named Elijah who talked with 850 prophets of another religion about who was the true and living God. He then asked one of the most profound questions known to mankind. "How long will you falter between two opinions?" (Islam, Judaism, Christianity, Buddhism, Scientology, Zoroastrianism, etc.)

Elijah then did what you and I should do. He proclaimed who God was by His name and what God would do by His word to prove Himself. The other 850 prophets did the same, but their gods couldn't perform like Elijah's God, who is the God of Abraham, Isaac and Jacob. The scriptures account that when the undecided people saw this they fell on their faces and proclaimed, "The Lord, He is God!" Why did the people say that? Its simple; God proved Himself!

How does God prove himself? Through a word called TRUTH. What does truth mean?

- Truth is a core set of facts that are consistent with reality.
- Most people confuse truth with opinion and the difference can be as far as the east is from the west.

There are some theologians that say Christians and Muslims serve the same God. The statement sounds warm, fuzzy, very mellifluous, but it couldn't be furthest from the truth.

The fact is the Quran and the Bible is like the distance between East and West. Ok writer, prove it!

Let's examine the Quran in contrast to the Holy Bible. Which writing closer bears the nature and character of God? Which book is divine versus human in nature?

Bible	Quran
I Corinthians 7:2:	Surat 33:50:
...Marry one wife	*Husbands marry up to four wives*
Ephesians 5:25:	Surat 4:34:
Husband love your wives...	*Husbands beat your wives (lightly)*
Matthew 5:39-47; Hebrews 12:14	Surat 9:29:
Love your enemies	*Fight those who don't believe in Islam*
Pray for your enemies	*Smite their necks until you have killed and wounded them*
Live peacefully among all people	
Bless those who despitefully use you	
John 14:9, Rev 1:8:	Surat 4:116:
I and the Father are one	*Allah do not forgive those who ascribe partners to Him*
I am the Alpha and Omega,	
The Almighty	
Revelations 21:4:	Surat 55:70-74:
In heaven there will be no more death crying or pain	*In heaven you will have 72 virgins*

(From the contrasting ideologies as a reasonable person can conclude the god of the Quran and the God of the Bible have totally distinct and opposing theologies.) Moreover, they are not just different but the exact opposite of each other.

So how do we determine who God is?

You determine who God is through a word called TRUTH. The truth was established through the miracles and wonders performed by God and His SON Jesus Christ. Why the miracles? Because the miracles He did, only an Almighty God could do; they confirmed who He said Jesus said they were and what they we able to do (I and the Father are one).

Here are a few examples:
1) Able to forgive sin, Mark 2:5
2) Able to raise the dead, Mark 5:35-42, John 11:1-46
3) Able to control the elements, Mark 4:39
4) Have demons submit, Mark 1:23-27
5) The Resurrection of Jesus, I Peter 1:3

When Jesus said in John 14:6 '*I am the way, the truth, the life*,' He validated His claim through the indisputable fact of the Resurrection. All other gods or so called "prophets" have died and are still dead. Only Jesus had the power to lay down His life and pick it back up. Therefore, I can have trust if He promises me that He s going to pull me out of a situation because he is God then nothing is impossible for Him (Luke 1:37).

.

9
WHAT'S SO SPECIAL ABOUT THAT JEWISH CARPENTER

While writing this book, I had a strange experience. While driving the country side, there was a pickup truck in front of me with a sticker on it that read *"A Jewish Carpenter Fixed All My Problems."* I knew and understood exactly who the sign was speaking of but why this particular Jewish Carpenter?

I want to share a bevy of different scenarios about different people at different times with totally distinct situations, who for some unforeseen reason, started to look for this Jewish Carpenter.

While surfing the internet, I ran across an article that read *Jailed W.T.C. Mastermind Ramzi Yusef Had a Mystery Conversion to Jesus the Christ* (while incarcerated at a super maximum prison in Florence, Colorado.) **Wow!** This conversion may be deeper than Apostle Paul's conversion. Here is a man that plotted to kill thousands of people but only managed to kill six people and injure 1400 innocent people. He was indicted for masterminding the bombing of an Iranian Shrine, the attempted assassination of Benazir Bhutto and the bombing of a Philippine Airline Flight 434. A man who at sentencing, a Federal Judge called an "apostle of evil," all of a sudden began worshipping a Jewish Carpenter.

The question that leaves a person hanging in the air is where is the rationale?

What was his motive? Ramzi is going to physically die in jail. He has no chance for parole. According to Islam, if a believer seeks another faith and converts to it, the penalty is death on this earth, and eternal hell fire. Surat 4:89. Moreover, his dream of reaching paradise and having sex with 72 virgins, coupled with his glorious reputation as a martyr in Islam is thrown out the window. So in essence, Ramzi Yousef gave up his whole being for a Jewish Carpenter that died 2000 years ago. Things that make you say hmmmm!

I once received a desperate phone call from a friend. We exchanged greetings and she explained why she was grieving extensively:

While ascending the steps to her home, she heard the sound of passionate love making coming from her basement. Her thinking was it was her son and daughter-in-law, since they resided there with her. She then proceeded to the area to gingerly tell the couple to hold the noise down; when to her shock and amazement, the daughter-in-law was caught in the act of adultery with her husband's best friend. When questioned how she could do such a despicable thing, she replied, "I need Jesus." The question is, why a Jewish Carpenter and why a Jewish Carpenter now? Right after a highly intense adulterous sexual tryst she called on a Jewish carpenter that died 2000 years ago!

Voodoo is a religion that was brought to the western coast by slaves from Africa. It is believed to have started in Haiti in 1724 as a snake cult that worshipped many spirits pertaining to daily life experiences. Voodoo belief recognizes one Supreme Being who created the universe, but who is too far away for a personal relationship with its worshippers. Therefore, the cult followers serve the lesser deities to gain guidance for their lives. The lesser are demonic spirits, spirits of animals, spirits of natural forces and spirits of good and evil.

Haiti is a nation that was reputed for embracing this religion. In 2010, one of the worst natural disasters happened in Haiti in the history of the world. Thousands of men women and children were killed, displaced, maimed and injured. Several days later, an aftershock hit Haiti. Men, women and children ran out their shelters screaming, "Jesus, help me! Jesus, help me!" and immediately the activity stopped. Why did the Haitians abandon their beliefs, and what made them call on a Jewish Carpenter that died over 2,000 years ago? Hmmmmm!

Without controversy, why would three different peoples from three different backgrounds call on this Jewish Carpenter that died 2,000 years ago? It is simple. The burdens of the problems of their hearts surpassed any solution that could be given through philosophy, religion, counseling, and the like. When you look at Ramzi, the Haitians, and the daughter-in-law their hearts cried out for something out of this world; something holy, pure, undefiled that could bring peace to their spirits. Therefore, for that reason they called on Jesus.

- Jesus asks this very important question: "Who do men say that I, the Son of Man, am?"

- Then he asks the ultimate question, "Who do you say that I am?"

When dealing with the subject of Christ, you're dealing with a Trilemma. Either He is a:
1. Liar
2. Lunatic
3. Lord

You see most people say He was a nice spiritual person, or a good prophet, but I disagree; because if He told humanity to trust in Him for salvation when He knew He wasn't God, then he would qualify to be the evilest person in history.

Additionally, if He presented Himself to be God in Israel knowing that the Jews are fiercely monotheistic, He would set himself up for suicide. Why wouldn't He do that in Egypt or Greece where they believe in polytheism (many gods) so He would be a Lunatic?

Or you can do like Ramzi, the Haitians and the daughter-in-law and call Him "Lord." You can recognize through the "eternity" that was placed in your heart that Jesus was not just a prophet, good guy or Jewish Carpenter, but was God incarnated.

Wait a minute Minister Lamont, the Bible only says that He was Gods only begotten Son. So aren't we all God's sons? The answer is no. There is a distinct difference between humans and Christ. When humans beget, they beget humans, when **God** begets, he begets God. Now while we can apprehend this mystery because we are finite beings, we cannot comprehend eternal things.

Therefore, when Ramzi, The Haitians and the daughter-in-law mysteriously started looking for the Jewish Carpenter, they all made a step in the right direction because when they began looking for the Carpenter, they all found God:

Is not this the carpenter's son? Is not his mother called Mary? And his brethren, James, and Joses, and Simon, and Judas? (Matthew 13:55)

I am Alpha and Omega, the beginning and the ending, saith the Lord, which is, and which was, and which is to come, the Almighty. (Revelations 1:8)

10
DON'T TRIP

As I was typing this portion of my manuscript, I overheard my son Lamont Jr. telling a person on the phone "Don't trip! Don't trip!" When he finished his phone call, I asked him, 'What does this "don't trip" thing mean?' He said in his cool language, "It sort of means don't let that stop you from doing what you do." I interpreted that as "don't let a stumbling block keep you from moving forward."

When most humans begin to worship God, they direct it to an image of God, instead of at God's person. That is why in the Book of Exodus 20:4 God says, *You shall not make a carved image or any likeness of anything that is in heaven above.* If the Bible is true and Christ is on the right hand of God, then to make imagery of Christ is disobedience to God.

If you ever observed most Caucasian people of any ethnic race, they are mostly Catholics. Why? Imagery. They see a Caucasian Jesus, Caucasian Angels, a Caucasian Mary and they immediately adopt the faith. Ask about the Trinity, law, prophet, Pauline Gospels, and they are clueless, but they confess that is what they are.

Conversely, African-Americans have flooded the doors of Islam. Ask about the Hadith, Sunna, Hijrah, the 5 pillars, etc. Most are lost. What is it that attracts most people about Islam?

There are no images of Mohammad.

When African Americans see European imagery, without examining the truth of God's word, they immediately reject him due to the longstanding, volatile relationship between blacks and whites. Recently, I was driving down the road and I saw a man that I knew for years. He was of another faith. I started to keep driving, but the spirit of the living God said, "Stop and tell this man about my Son." I pulled over, and I called the gentleman by name. As we began to exchange pleasantries, I revealed to him that I was born again. He must have jumped backwards twenty feet. He looked at me with disdain, and when I asked what was wrong he replied, "Oh, the same white man that put you in slavery is the same white man you trust for salvation?" As I began to give my reason for hope, he walked away angrily. This man was an 82 year old man. It is highly likely that this man will die in his sins.

Although there are many people who agree with this man's ideology, if you examine what he said closely you will conclude that it is flawed. First, if you study African History and not use the movie "Roots" and "Amistad" as your standard you will see that it wasn't Europeans who first put Africans in slavery. Africans themselves put other Africans in slavery and opened the door for other races to pillage Africans physically and mentally. Additionally, for every African slave brought to the United States, many more were abducted by Arabs from North Africa, Arabia and the Middle East. Logic would then expect to find many times more descendants of slaves living today in North Africa, Arabia and the Middle East as found in America.

Today some thirty million descendants of African slaves reside in America today, where there are perhaps thirty million descendants of African slaves that should be residing over North Africa, the Middle East and Arabia today. Why are they nowhere to be found or seen? The grim horror is that Arab slavers customarily castrated black males that they captured. Why? So no black man could ever be a sexual threat to Arab women in North African households. Arab slaveholders denied male Africans freedom of wages, but even worse, the sacred human privileges of marriage, sex and parenting.

If you do personal study and not just swallow the whole Encyclopedia Britannica and National Geographic magazine that hide the well-known truth about black elders across the Sub-Saharan Africa, you will find evidence that supports that Arab slave owners did indeed step in to do what the emasculated black males could not. Tens of millions of brown skinned people descended from the offspring of Arab mothers and fathers found all across North Africa and the Middle East.

What message am I trying to convey? Am I taking the focus off the Europeans? God Forbid. The answer is no. What I am attempting to illustrate is slavery itself is dead wrong. The Bible condemns it in I Timothy 1:10 where it says, *"No Slaver or Kidnapper will see the kingdom of God.*" Whether the Slaver is Caucasian or Arab, the crime is horrendous. What's telling is because of the imagery of Jesus depicted as a Caucasian, most Africans as well as African Americans have not only stumbled at the cross, but have deleted the Arabs out of one of the worst indictments in history. Incidentally, the crime that happened 400 years ago in West Africa is still being acted out this very day in Sudan and you won't hear a peep from the African or Afro-American community or their leaders.

I said all this to illustrate that this black man with an Arab name, who spoke Arabic, stumbled so hard at the imagery of Jesus Christ, that he not only didn't know his history with respects to his holocaust, but he with great joy learned how to speak his oppressors language and culture with pride. He never even acknowledged the first actors who started the holocaust train, which were indigenous Africans and Arabs.

This man suffered from two things. He was a sinner and never wanted to come under the moral strictures of scripture because it would cause him to stop what he loved and that is sin. Also, he had intractable difficulties believing in a God that he couldn't relate to ethnically, one whom caused him to think of the negative experiences caused by race. With the two problems, he used the race card to support the fact that he enjoyed a life of sin and didn't want to change. Without the trump card of imagery, he wouldn't have a case to bring to a jury.

I have run into countless situations like this one, which caused me to go where no man has gone before with respects to the physical image of Jesus. Put your seatbelts on!
Let's examine man's theology. Well, since most Jews are European we will portray Christ as European. What color were the Jews prior to the Diaspora? And are there Jews of every ethnic race today? - Indian, black, Spanish, etc.? Okay then, let's look at it from an Afro centric perspective. He had to be Black because when the angel told Joseph to go hide Christ why did he tell him to hide Christ in Egypt. Why didn't the angel say go hide him in Poland or Switzerland, so he had to be black right, right? When you look in the Book of Revelations, it says that Christ's hair was like wool and feet was like burnt brass. What color is burnt brass? – Dark. What race's hair is like wool? Black people! Case closed! Christ was Black!

As plausible as this dissertation seems, none of it is true! Let's examine Christ from a Biblical perspective. In Isaiah 53:2, scripture says that Christ had no beauty and his face was marred more than any man. Correct me if I am wrong because I have a teachable spirit but Christ may have been the most unattractive undesirable man to look at on the face of the earth according to scripture. In Acts 17:29, God said that we ought not to think that the divine nature of God is anything shaped by art or man's devising. Then he goes on to say in verse 30, "Truly, these times of ignorance are overlooked, but now God wants all men to repent."

Last but not least, Revelations 1:8-15. Most people of color use this scripture as counter racism as a response to Jesus being portrayed in movies, art and churches as White, but sadly this scripture has been misinterpreted. Okay, I'll prove it by examining the scripture. Who wrote Revelations? God! Who did God use to transcribe it? Apostle John. When John wrote Revelations was he talking about the Jesus that walked the earth with him or the glorified Jesus whom we are awaiting now? It was the glorified Jesus.

When John described Jesus did he describe Him literally or symbolically? He described Him symbolically. What were the symbols? - Majesty and judgment:
- Clothed with garment down to the feet… Flowing robes are a token of dignity.
- Hair white like wool – Symbolizes eternity he is of Ancient days
- Eyes as a flame – symbolizes bring hidden things to past.
- Voice as the sound of many – power and majesty.
- Countenance – As the sunshine in its strength. Shekinah Glory
- Feet like burnt brass – brass symbolizes judgment - not **ethnicity!**

"God is a spirit and those who worship Him must worship Him in Spirit and in truth." God transcends nationalism, racism and the like. This is why he says in Jeremiah 32:27, *I am the God of all flesh*, and He supports this in the New Testament by saying, *There is neither Jew, non Jew, slave, Scythian…Christ is all and in all.*

I had the experience of preaching to a congregation of mixed races. What was so comforting was that as I watched Asians, Africans, Europeans, and all diverse races walk through the door, there was a spirit of authority and justification in the church. Every soul in the place felt as though God was a part of them. Why? No imagery, just the Word of God!

11
GOD DON'T HAVE NO PARTNERS

In most faiths, the "Trinity" is an incomprehensible mystery and is dismissed as fallacy. Jehovah's Witnesses say the "Trinity" is a freakish three headed monster, and Muslims say that God doesn't have any partners. The Muslims are right: God doesn't have any partners, but He does have Persons.

It is important to understand when Trinitarians speak of the trinity, they are speaking of the nature and essence of one God with three persons that all are externally distinct.

The Father (the Creator) is 100% God. God the Son who is the Redeemer is 100% God. The Holy Spirit who is the converter, who teaches you about God, is 100% God. It makes perfect sense when you analyze the concept of the Trinity.

The Muslims are correct; God is sovereign, all mighty, undefiled, and purely holy. If that be true (and it is,) then how could this holy, just, pure, sovereign, undefiled God commune with an unholy, unjust, finite, sinful race of people? He can't. So how does

He compensate? He emptied Himself of His glory and begot a Son. Beget does not mean beginning nor through sexual relations. It means that a part of God's person emptied Himself of His glory to become human flesh and yet remained 100% Deity (that's what Christ exemplified in His earthly ministry by doing miracles that only God can do.)

A man can mediate between two men, but he cannot mediate between a man and a horse – because he has not the nature of both a man and horse. So the unique only begotten Son of God could not mediate between God and man until he became the GOD MAN, by his virgin birth, born of the Holy Spirit and a woman or human. He not only became a man, but it was necessary that he took his human nature back to heaven with Him, to make intercession on humanity's behalf.

Example:
Let's presuppose all humanity were ants and their mission in life was to walk straight - but every single ant walked crooked. Now this poses a dilemma for the Almighty. How could the Almighty get ants to walk straight?

Could he first yell from out of heaven, saying in a loud voice, "Walk straight?" Logically that would not work because since the nature of God is straight and the nature of the ant is crooked, the ant could never comprehend.

Could God then come out of heaven and become an ant (since nothing is impossible for God?) That wouldn't work either. By God becoming an ant, he would have the crooked nature of the ant, and he couldn't show the ant how to walk straight.

Now if God stepped out of heaven, became an ant and maintained his deity, could He then teach ants how to walk straight? The answer, logically, is a resounding YES!

Then there is the Holy Spirit that convicts humans and reveals they need a SAVIOR. He Himself brings humans to Christ for the purpose of salvation. So, is the Holy Spirit a person? The answer is yes!

- Romans 8:26 - the Holy Spirit is described as a pronoun (Himself)
- Ephesians 4:30 - the Holy Spirit is described as being grieved, so clearly scripture aptly codifies that the Holy Spirit is a person.

The Jews asked, "How can a person be filled with another person?" That's a fairly reasonable question! My response is the Holy Spirit is not spatial but relational. Asking spatial questions about a being that has no extension in space makes as much sense as asking, what does the color blue taste like?

Then you have God the Father, purely holy, sinless, merciful, full of glory, all wise, all powerful, eternal, and one in essence.

Is this concept difficult to comprehend? Yes, because as finite beings, it is impossible to comprehend the infinite. The Trinity is apprehendable but comprehendible it is virtually impossible. Only by faith does God reveal this mystery to humans in part, and not exhaustively.

In Islamic theology, Muslims recoil at the notion of God having a Son or acknowledging God as a Father (Surratt 19:35, Surratt 6:101 and Sura 2:116). Even some of the forefathers of the United States had insuperable difficulty understanding the trinity, specifically Thomas Jefferson and Abraham Lincoln. Nevertheless, although it's a mystery with elements beyond understanding, it is not blasphemous or contradictory.

Scripture says God is the same today, yesterday and forever. The Trinity never changed from the Old Testament to the New Testament:

Let us make man in our image and in our likeness. (Genesis 1:26)

- Who was God speaking to? – Himself, the Holy Spirit and His Son.

And I will pour upon the house of David, and upon the inhabitants of Jerusalem, the spirit of grace and of supplications: and they shall look upon me whom they have pierced, and they shall mourn for him, as one mourneth for his only son, and shall be in bitterness for him, as one that is in bitterness for his firstborn. (Zechariah 12:10)

- Who is the "I" in this verse? - God Almighty!

- What is the Spirit of Grace? - The Holy Spirit.

- Who did they pierce? Jesus the Christ, on the cross.

What's telling is this Old Testament prophecy of the Trinity is 600 years before Christ:

Isaiah 49:16, *The Lord God and His Spirit has sent Me.* When Scripture is capitalized in the Old Testament and New Testament, it indicates Deity. Who is the ME in this verse? – Jesus, the Christ.

The Quran is accurate, *God doesn't have any partners,* but He does have three distinct persons in nature and essence. The Father is fully God, The Son is fully God, and the Holy Spirit is fully God. The Bible presents one "What" and three "Who's." Well, why wouldn't God speak to humans exhaustively about His nature? Think about this carefully, **if God was small enough to comprehend, would He be big enough to worship?**

12
THE PROOF IS IN THE PUDDING

I would like to use some significant historical events in U.S. history: slavery / the Civil War & the election of the first African American president to draw a corollary. Warning! You may not agree with my theology, but I guarantee it will cause you to think differently about the truth of who God is.

If you've ever had the opportunity to watch the movie "Roots" or "Amistad," you will observe some of the most heinous crimes in the history of humanity - the Trans Atlantic Slave Trade. If you can stomach it, you will see Africans kidnapped, beat, raped, psychologically tortured and last but not least killed in various manners. At some point if you watch objectively, these slaves began to look for God. Their main religion was Islam because before Europeans were apprised of the lucrative nature of slave trading, Arab Muslims were well advanced in slave trading. During the Arab occupation, most Africans learned the Islamic religion or they choose to worship dumb idols.

Now there came a point where the Africans' cry was so extreme that it hit heaven. God answered and punished their European oppressors through the American Civil War. You want me to prove it? I will delight in doing so! In the United States, Southern insistence on perpetuating slavery and Northern opposition to it contributed to a bloody civil war in which 600,000 men died and two million others were seriously wounded. The ten year long war in South Vietnam took 58,000 American lives, yet just one three day battle at Gettysburg killed at least 51,000. That had to be the hand of God showing His displeasure for the cruelty perpetuated on the Africans.

Which God did they call on? Was it Confucius, was it the Virgin Mary? Was it Buddha? Was it one of the 100 Hindu gods? Was it Allah, or was it JESUS? If you study your history carefully, it was Jesus.

For years, I was under the thinking that the White House was for White people, and it was a fallacy to think that an African American could succeed as President. What's telling is even now as a man of faith, my thinking hadn't changed. I actually accepted it as an immutable fact without regard to Luke 1:37 *"For with God nothing will be impossible!"*

As I watched the campaign unfold, I observed Barack Obama's demeanor, decorum, and his genius. This man did not use the predictable garden variety tactics that most of his African American predecessors used, such as slavery, reparations and the injustices of America - tactics that failed overwhelmingly. He moved as if God Himself was directing his steps. He said, "We can do it. Together, we can build a nation." His battle cry was unity, not dissention. Twenty two months later at Barack Obama's inauguration, he paid homage (honor and respect) to everyone's religion, even atheists, but he confirmed that it was the God of the Bible that exalted him, Jesus the Christ.

I believe my theory will be debated vigorously, but you cannot debate the results. God is always a God that proves He is God, evidenced by results.

The proof is in the pudding!

Let every soul be subject unto the higher powers. For there is no power but of God: the powers that be are ordained of God. (Romans 13:1)

Thus saith the LORD the King of Israel, and his redeemer the LORD of hosts; I am the first, and I am the last; and beside me there is no God. (6).

And who, as I, shall call, and shall declare it, and set it in order for me, since I appointed the ancient people? and the things that are coming, and shall come, let them shew unto them. (7).

Fear ye not, neither be afraid: have not I told thee from that time, and have declared it? ye are even my witnesses. Is there a God beside me? yea, there is no God; I know not any. (8). (Isaiah 44:6-8)

While I do agree that the God of the Bible did elevate Barack Obama to the office of President of the United States, I am not in agreement with all of his political policies.

13
HOW DO I PRAY EFFECTIVELY

First, we must understand that prayer is a means of communicating with a Holy God, through simple conversation.

What do I mean by a "Holy God?"
- He is totally righteous.
- He knows all things.
- He knows your heart's intentions.
- He cannot be bribed or blackmailed.
- He is Sovereign.
- His ways are not easy to always comprehend.
- He does not bless sin.

To this end, when you approach Him you must reverence Him:

God commands this of Moses in Exodus 3:5:
Draw not nigh hither: put off thy shoes from off thy feet, for the place whereon thou standest is holy ground.

Now if God's presence makes dirty ground holy, how much holier is Almighty God Himself?

Now let's look at some keys facts that make prayer effective:

1. Secret prayer. Whenever Jesus prayed, He always withdrew to a lonely place to call upon God. Hypocrites seek glory through praying publically, babbling vain repetitions; this type of prayer repulses God because it is empty and worthless.

2. Recognize there is a connection between prayer and meditation. Our prayers are only as inspired as our intake of scripture. Scripture feeds meditation and meditation gives food to our prayers.

3. Hallow God. When a person hallows God, he or she distinguishes Almighty God from any other gods and his or her prayers tell what they believe Him for.

Example:
About 3,000 years ago in Israel, a king named Jehoshaphat heard disturbing news that three vicious armies were about to attack the nation of Israel and he prayed this prayer (in the presence of the nation):

O LORD God of our fathers, art not thou God in heaven? and rulest not thou over all the kingdoms of the heathen? And in thine hand is there not power and might, so that none is able to withstand thee? II Chronicles 20:6.

Wow!

So Jehoshaphat identified who God was, where He was located, and what he believed God for! That prayer, needed for Israel, not only defeated three enemies but also kept them from losing their possessions.

4. If you have ever studied Quantum Physics, you have

learned that sound changes the atmosphere. Every time I sing, shout, or clap, especially if I do so in a spiritual setting, the atmosphere shifts; whenever the atmosphere shifts, it creates a climate for a miracle.

Example:

If you ever study the gospel accounts where Jesus performed miracles, there was always an atmosphere set for the possibility of a miracle.

In Mark 10:46-52, Jesus was walking by Jericho with His disciples, and a beggar named blind Bartimaeus heard that he came by. He began to call out for Jesus, and many told him that he should remain quiet, but he cried out all the more, and scripture says that Jesus stood still and called him over. Jesus then asked *'What in the world do you want ME to do?'* In other words, *you name it.* He asked for his sight. Jesus said unto him, *'Go thy way thy faith has made you whole!'* Immediately he received his sight.

I wonder what would have happened if he kept his mouth shut!

5. Diligent prayer. This happens when a person prays and no matter how difficult things get, they are determined to believe.

Why is it called diligent prayer?

In Hebrews 11:6, the Bible sets the condition, *it is impossible to please God without faith; anyone who comes to God must first believe that He is God and that he is a rewarder of those who diligently seek him.*

The operative words in the text are REWARDER and DILIGENT. Faith is not just asking God for something, you receive it and you thank Him for it - that is a natural response. God is supernatural, so in order to please Him, you must operate in the realm of supernatural thought - Car repossessed? Lord I praise you! Terminated from your Job? Lord I praise you! Lien on your home, Lord I praise you! Cancer went to Stage III? Lord I praise you! H.I.V. turned to AIDS? Lord I praise you! Husband or wife had a baby outside of your marriage? Lord I praise you!

Seem weird? Absolutely! Actually it sounds absurd, but if you knew the hidden mystery behind it, your mind would be blown. Here is the mystery:

This is the will of God, in everything give thanks. (I Thessalonians 5:18)

I once had Bible Study with a gentleman that was a paraplegic. While underway, he said "I thank God for this wheelchair and my condition according to I Thessalonians 5:18." I responded, 'You're crazy!' He responded "Isn't that what the scripture says?" I responded 'No! It says ...***in all things give thanks***, not "*for all things*!' To praise God in an adverse condition demonstrates that your love for God is unconditional. Understand that God inhabits our lives where praise is, so if he is in the atmospheric realm, then whatever you believe for has to change. Whenever God shows up, so does change.

About two years ago, I met a young lady that told me her company was laying off workers. She asked me to pray for her. We touched and agreed, feeding her prayer with scripture and then stood in faith. One week later she walked into her office and found a pink slip on her desk. We ran into each other soon after. As I walked by, I greeted her 'Praise the Lord!' She tearfully responded "Praise the Lord!" She explained what happened and at the end of the conversation she said, "It's cool, I still believe God." She was making $30,000 a year on her former job.

One month later she called me and all I could hear was "God is Good" about ten times. She then gave her testimony:

One Friday she met her sister at TGI Friday's restaurant on City Line Avenue in Philadelphia, PA. While eating, her sister attempted to encourage her saying, "God didn't forget you." Moments later, she goes to the bathroom and runs into a college sorority sister / former roommate, Sylvia fixing her contact lens. They hug and get reacquainted. She asks, "Girl what brings you here?" Sylvia replies "My co-workers are throwing me a party because I just got a big promotion on my job. I am the head of human resources for a Fortune 500 company." She then informs Sylvia "I just got laid off." Sylvia gives her a business card and tells her to call her, so she can see what she can do. Two weeks later, she had an interview with the company. Today she is making $90,000 a year. God allowed her to get laid off so he could triple her salary.

What would have happened if she stopped believing?

So, the next time you pray and use the word AMEN, understand it is not a word used universally to say I'm signing off; put another way, it's also meant to say "Be it in accordance to your perfect counsel (oh Lord)." In the counsel of God, He doesn't want you to pray, "God move the mountain." The prayer he delights in is, "Give me the strength to climb!"

Why not just ask to move the mountain? Simple, God saw the mountain before it became your obstacle, and it's there to provoke you to do something with Him that he wants (your entire life.) Do you know what that is? **Have a conversation!** All he wants is a simple, intimate conversation that will ultimately lead to a relationship.

Why won't God answer prayer just like that? It's simple, you would stop talking to Him!

Let's look at another important aspect surrounding prayer. It's a must that you believe in angels to understand how God performs miracles. The study of biology helps you see that humans have a D.N.A. structure in the shape of a ladder called a double helix. If you read Genesis 28:12 and John 1:51, the Bible speaks about angels ascending and descending up and down Jacobs ladder. The question that begs to be answered is why are these angels ascending and descending up and down this ladder? The answer is this; when your prayers are communicated to God, they are answered by an agency of angels called "the Lord's Hosts."

Jacob's ladder, in the Bible, is an illustration of man communicating his desires to God through prayer. God, through the counsel of his will, in turn sends angels to answer prayers. God's system for doing things is fail proof. It is why He speaks so confidently about His promises in the Book of Isaiah 55:8-11:

For my thoughts are not your thoughts, neither are your ways my ways, saith the LORD.

For as the heavens are higher than the earth, so are my ways higher than your ways, and my thoughts than your thoughts.

For as the rain cometh down, and the snow from heaven, and returneth not thither, but watereth the earth, and maketh it bring forth and bud, that it may give seed to the sower, and bread to the eater:

So shall my word be that goeth forth out of my mouth: it shall not return unto me void, but it shall accomplish that which I please, and it shall prosper in the thing whereto I sent it.

Approximately ten years ago, a dear friend of mine was contemplating suicide because her boyfriend of four years left her for another woman. She couldn't eat or sleep. Worrying about this man was taking a toll on her life very much like a self-inflicted suicide attempt could. I felt really bad, because she was surrounded by a multitude of counselors who were not in touch with her infirmities. They would respond to her saying things like, "Oh forget him, you will get another one." Or "Men are like buses you miss one bus, another one is coming." This woman had been in a monogamous relationship where she was having sex. When you have sex or intimacy, you exchange D.N.A. through body fluids, and during that exchange that D.N.A. drops into your spirit. So what her counselors did not know was that a part of that man was in her actual spirit to the extent when he physically broke it off, part of her was physically dying. This is why God says in I Thessalonians, *Flee from fornication.*

Nevertheless, I prayed with my friend, and she asked God to please stop the pain and bring him back. Well, God being wise knew that this man was not a good for her.
One night shortly after she prayed, a commercial came on T.V. about a particular brand of ice cream. Well, she couldn't get the ice

cream off her mind. She called her girlfriend and said, "Come go with me to Pathmark. I want some ice cream." Moments later her girlfriend pulled up and the two of them went to Pathmark supermarket. While traveling through the aisles, she noticed a tall, muscular male with green eyes. She said to her girlfriend, "Wow! Was he gorgeous! He looked like he just dropped from heaven!" Moments later, they both ran into one another at the frozen food section. Guess what the young man was shopping for? Ice cream!

They began to converse. She told him about the ice cream commercial; they both revealed they were hurt by their partners and had asked God to take away the pain. From that encounter, they dated and are now married. Isn't it ironic to know that the man who caused my friend all the pain eventually stalked her?

When you look at the science of statistical data what are the odds two people going through the same thing, meeting in a supermarket in the ice cream section at a peculiar hour, craving for the same ice cream after praying the same prayer - and it gets answered? After racking your brains attempting to think of a reason, recognize that it all leads back to God working through an agency of angels; God honoring prior conversations two parties had with Him.

And this is the confidence we have in him, that, if we ask anything according to his will, he heareth us:

And if we know that he hears us, whatsoever we ask, we know that we have the petitions that we desired of him.

I John 5:14-15

14
HOW CAN I BE CERTAIN GOD IS ANSWERING MY PRAYERS

This is a question that even a mature minister, pastor, and bishop struggle with but the struggle is over. First, we know and understand that God answers prayers three ways:

1. No,
2. Yes
3. Wait.

Second, we know according to 1 John 5:14,15 that we can have confidence that He hears and answers all our prayers, but God strives to get the believer who is weak in faith to believe by fact. What do I mean? The Bible says we walk by faith and not by sight. That's very true but have you read Judges 6:36-40 or Isaiah 53:1 or the four synoptic Gospels?

How do these scriptures tie in to my point? It's simple.

Let's deal with the first character Gideon in the Book of Judges

Chapter 6. Throughout the chapter, through Gideon's entire tribulation, He didn't just say "Help me Jehovah, I trust you, Amen." Instead, he asked God for a sign. A sign is something physical. If you believe in the true and living God of the Bible, then you must believe in angels. Angels are spiritual agents that God used to perform miracles, and when you have a relationship with God, the angels are encamped around you. Although metaphysical, they cause physical realities like your prayers to be answered. If you are pondering in your head whether or not God is answering your prayers and you asked for a sign, that angelic host will cause something to give you a sign to comfort you while God is manifesting your prayer.

Example:

Two years ago, I was in prayer about a very serious, personal matter. Although God had performed enough miracles in my life already for me to believe, I was struggling in faith, so I asked God to give me a sign. Ten minutes later, a white dove appeared at my window. You might say so what. I say different. First, I have lived at the residence for approximately 25 years and never saw a white dove. The dove is the sign of the Holy Spirit. Also, doves are very uncommon in this region, especially in the dead of winter in ten degree weather. After logical deduction I concluded:

1. I prayed for a sign
2. 10 minutes later a dove appeared
3. Doves are a sign of the Holy Spirit
4. Doves are uncommon in the region. Doves are almost never seen in weather below 40 degrees. It was 10 degrees.

With all of those factors, it had to be God. Additionally, my prayer was answered two days later.

When the Bible asks *who has the Arm of Lord been revealed to* this is a prophecy about God's people. Over 2,000 years ago, Almighty God stepped out of heaven travelled through the cosmos and manifested Himself in the person of Jesus Christ of Nazareth. What geographical location did God come to? Israel and never stepped outside of Israel during His ministry. So Jesus was *the Arm of the Lord who was revealed.* How did he reveal Himself? - Through signs and wonders. Actually, the Jews were foretold by Moses in Deuteronomy 18:15 that this person was coming and how Israel would identify Him. According to Moses, He would be Jewish and like him He would perform signs and wonders.

If you read Matthew, Mark, Luke and John, the Jews not only lived by faith but they also lived by sight. They physically had God with them (Immanuel = God with us) and still didn't believe. We physically have God in us (the Holy Spirit) but sometimes need a physical move of God to help us with our unbelief.

Have you ever read Psalm 37:23? *The steps of a good man are ordered by the Lord.* How does God order man's steps? Through signs and wonders. In Proverbs 3:5, 6 why would you acknowledge God, and how would God give you receipt that you acknowledged Him? Through signs and wonders.

If you don't have to lean on blind faith alone, put in another way, we live on faith based on facts. If that be true and it is, your prayers are answered 100% of the time.

15
CAN GOD TURN MY TRAGEDY INTO TRIUMPH

The Bible says in Luke 1:37: *For with God nothing is impossible.* Actually storms and mountains (big problems) are the very things that attract God's presence. You see, your tragedy was a divine set up. You were set up to be blessed. How can I say that when you're going through pure hell? Easy, because twelve years ago I was caught up in a serious tragedy (that I will discuss further on in this book) and it felt as though I would never come out, but Almighty God turned my tragedy into triumph. Actually, you may have naysayers, hoping that you don't come out, predicting that you are finished. That is when God shows Himself *BIG!* God adores the underdog. He said in James 2:5, *Didn't God chose the poor of this world (the nobodies) to be rich in faith?* Poor is not just a financial state, but mental and emotional also.

There was a man named Joseph in the Bible whose brothers were very jealous of his looks, his gift of interpreting dreams and the favor that his parents had for him. One day while his brothers went to feed their father's sheep, they secretly conspired to kill him, and say some wild beast attacked and killed him. His brother Reuben altered the plan, so Joseph would just be cast in a pit alive. Judah had a better plan and said let's sell him to the Arabs, dip his tunic into animal blood so his father would think that Joseph died by an animal ripping him apart. As fate would have it, they pulled Joseph out of the hole and sold him for 20 lousy shekels.

What they didn't know was what they meant for evil, God meant for good, and that is exactly what you may be dealing with now. You may be in a place where your whole world is turned upside down and people have wronged you are hoping for a negative outcome, but what they don't know is that God is taking that occasion of evil against you that has you in the pit, to elevate you to the palace.

You see, as the story goes on, the Arabs sold Joseph to an esteemed man named Potiphar, an officer of Pharaoh. The Lord was with Joseph and made him successful in the Egyptians house (look at God's hand!) and the Egyptian put everything he had in Joseph's authority. There came a time when there was a famine in Israel, and Joseph's brothers had to come to Joseph who at this time was the vice President of Egypt; which Egypt encompassed a great portion of the entire world. So yes, God always turns your tragedy into triumph. That is how He gets His glory, through the "nobodies" of the world, the forgotten people and the destitute people. If Joseph's brothers wouldn't have put him in the pit, then God most likely wouldn't have put him in the palace.

Blessed are you who hunger now for you shall be filled, blessed are you who weep now, for you shall laugh.

You'll Never Know God Is All You Need Until You Realize God is All You Have

(Luke 6:21)

16
IF GOD COULD ANSWER THE DEVIL'S PRAYER I KOW HE WILL ANSWER MINE

One night while writing this book, I stumbled across a chapter in the Bible that I must have read at least a hundred times; Luke 7:26-39. Since the Word of God is a living word, I was not surprised that God gave me a revelation in the chapter, because it has happened to me several times. But this special revelation shook my theology and very well may shake yours also.

What motivated me to write this chapter was I was hearing from a consortium of believers whose prayers God didn't answer. I turn on the radio, God didn't answer my prayer; I go online, God didn't answer my prayer; different ministries, God didn't answer my prayer. I knew that the people were "testa-lying," and not truthfully testifying. When one testifies, in our system of justice, it is expected that what comes forth from their mouths is truth, so a matter can be dealt with properly.

God answers prayers three ways:
1. No!
2. Yes!
3. Wait!

Oftentimes, *"No,"* or *"Wait"* can be misinterpreted as a "No" response for unanswered prayer. To those who hold fast to this tenet, this chapter should reassure you that God answers prayer.

When I think of God and the devil, I see two extremes: the devil as the personification of evil and God the personification of good. Therefore, when I saw the devil pray in Luke 7 and get answered, my mind was blown away. When Jesus approached these demons named "Legion," unlike most believers the demons first fell down before Christ, demonstrates extreme humility, and addressed him as Jesus, Son of the Most High God demonstrating a hallowing or deep intellectual respect for the person of Christ - God in the flesh. The scripture says the demons begged or implored Christ not to send them in the Abyss, but into the swine.

Now you might ask what the Abyss is? In the New Testament, the Abyss is the abode of the imprisoned demons not to be distinguished with Hades, the Lake of Fire or Tartarus (the prison for fallen angels). Put another way, it is the primeval ocean or the unfathomable bottomless pit that the evil spirits did not want to go to before their predetermined time.

Jesus answered their prayers and sent them into the swine. Now if God will answer a demon, there is no way on earth that He won't answer a believer who is made in His image and likeness, redeemed by His own blood and justified by covenants. The devil represents none of these, and Christ answered the demon's prayer. Believers have all of the three when we confess Christ as Savior and Lord, and **yet *can still doubt*** God for answered prayer.

The next time you hear someone say that God didn't answer their prayer, you make sure you respond by saying, "If he answered devil's, He has to answer mine!"

17
GO THY WAY, AS THOU HAS BELIEVED

In Matthew 8:5-13, Jesus entered an affluent city called Capernaum where He encountered a centurion whom begged Him to heal his servant. What's unique about the story was Jesus was very willing to answer the centurion's prayer quickly. Why? When he first approached Jesus, he called Him Lord, which is the equivalent of saying Jehovah or God. The centurion was not our ordinary man; he was in command of hundreds of men. When he called Jesus Lord, by faith he told Him "I believe you have authority over anything and everything that has come into existence." When Jesus saw his faith, He consented to come heal the man's servant, but the way scripture reads, it didn't appear that Jesus was going with lights and sirens, but then something happened. The man bumped his faith up a notch which caused Jesus to turn on lights and sirens. Here's what's significant about the centurion and his faith:

The man told Jesus that although he was a man of authority, he knew what "authority" was. Then he told Him He didn't have to come to his house like He did the rest of the people (the Jews); just Speak the Word, and he would believe that his servant would be healed. That faith confession blew Jesus' mind. Jesus said, "Wow,

I haven't found such great faith in Israel, nor, I have I seen such faith in the church!" What did Jesus mean by this comment? The Jewish Bible (Old Testament) foretold of Jesus over three hundred times, then He came in the flesh and performed what the prophecy spoke and they still refused to believe. Here's a man, a non-Jew, and stranger of the Bible, who not only had faith, but great faith.

Jesus' response, "Go thy way, and as thou hast believed, so let it be done to thee."

This is exactly what God is saying to you, the reader, *"As you have believed, let it be done to you."*

18
CUT ME IN, OR CUT IT OUT

...Just Existing

One day, I was talking with a friend of the man who raised me, Jeremiah Shabazz. As we rehashed old times, he used a term frequently used by gangsters involved in extortion which is "Cut me in, or cut it out!" The term means *"if you are making money legally or illegally either you give me a share of your proceeds or stop doing business."*
As I began to meditate on that meeting, as secular and ungodly as the statement was, it did have significance pertaining to the Kingdom of God.

How many people do you know in the kingdom of God and outside that are just existing - with no purpose, dreams, visions; just a bump on a log? That has to be one of the most miserable states a person can be in. The world and the church are full of them. I know, I used to be one of them, but at some point I developed the same mentality as the gangsters *"Cut me in or cut it out."*

You may say, "Lamont I think you are being prideful and misunderstanding the scriptures!" At first glance, it may appear that I am. But with close, careful examination, you will see that I am in rapt harmony with the scriptures. Let's examine a scripture where a man (like you and me) pressed God and essentially told Him to *"cut me in, or cut it out."*

Gen 32:24:
Then Jacob was left alone and a man (God) wrestled with him until the breaking of day. Now when God saw that he could not prevail against him, he touched the socket of his hip, and the socket was out of joint as he wrestled with him. And he (God) said, "Let me go, for the day breaks." But he said, I will not let you go unless you bless me. So he (God) said to him what is your name? He said Jacob. And He (God) said your name shall no longer be Jacob, but Israel, for you have struggled with God and with men and have prevailed and God blessed him right there.

This scripture is fraught with mysteries that speaking frankly I haven't discerned. One thing that I have discerned is that Jacob pressed God so hard that God gave up. At a certain point, that press became so intense that God touched the socket of Jacob's hip and it became disjointed. Then when Jacob pressed forward even more God almighty gave up. What is the first thing God did for Jacob after Jacobs's victory? He changed his name.

Whenever a person comes into the presence of God, something always changes.

In the Book of Exodus 3:5, God told Moses to take his sandals off because the place where he stood was holy ground. It was God's presence that made a filthy dirty desert ground holy.

When God shows up, something must change.

One of the greatest stories in the Bible that points to people "just existing" is when the children of Israel wandered in the wilderness for forty years. I looked up the word "wander" and it means *to move about without fixed course, aim or goal, to go idly about, to walk a place with no intention to go into a particular direction.* Why did the children of Israel walk around the wilderness for forty years? Simple, God revealed his power and majesty through great signs and wonders and they refused to believe him.

Now the question today for you the reader is, are you just existing with no purpose, and if so, why? Are you on the same job with no promotion? Are you living from pay check to pay check? Are you going from one bad relationship to another? Do you go into worship and leave out the same way you come in (stressed)? If you died today, would your legacy be that of a person who made things happen or just someone who never snatched God in the collar and said, *"Cut me in, or cut it out.* I know I will come under intense scrutiny, but the Bible is clear in Hebrews 4:15 where it says "...come boldly to the throne of grace in the time of need." Tears and whining never moves the hand of God, only faith! In the Book of Ecclesiastes, the Bible says *to everything there is a season, a time for every purpose under heaven.* Why is it always a negative season in your life? - Why are there always poverty, heartaches, issues, and stress? When do these issues drive you to say, *Cut me in?*

Whenever a person presses into God, there is always a shift in the atmosphere. I recently attended a church in Camden, N.J., Voice of Hope Deliverance. When I walked into the church, it was dark and quiet. It was sort of a culture shock, because I've never experienced that before. When worship began, it was so intense that it appeared that the worship leader brought God in by the hand. When it finally was time for the minister to give the Word of God, the atmosphere had shifted from natural to the supernatural and in its appearance, the believers were experiencing breakthroughs.

On January 26, 2013 at 10:30 AM, I had my own personal wrestling match with God; there are witnesses to verify this story. On January 25, my sister Sarah R. McLaurin was down with the flu. Most people can catch the flu, and it's not an alarming situation, but she is an insulin dependent diabetic. The common flu for her can be fatal. I spoke to my sister around 1:00 PM that day. She was sickly, but I thought she would pull through. That night the rest of my family and I made a mistake that proved to be critical, we didn't' check on her. Approximately 10:15 AM, my older sister

Marilyn called and asked if I heard from Sarah. I said 'No,' and immediately fear and concern dropped into my spirit. I then called her son Tyler to see if he spoke to her and he said "No." He called several times, but the phone kept ringing. When he said that, common sense said that she was dead.

I proceeded to her house and knocked on the door; the smell of death was in the atmosphere. I then called 911 for assistance, and the police entered through a window. When I walked through her hallway, I knew she was physically dead. The police officer went in first and by his reaction when he came out, I just knew she went to be with the Lord. I entered her bedroom, and as I expected I found her lifeless body lying across the bed, with yellow foam excreting from her mouth. I went into a deep trance and began to wrestle with God; I would not accept my sister's present condition. I began calling God by an Old Testament name *El, Elyon, Elohim*, the self-existent one, *The Great I Am*. As I began wrestling in the spirit, it seemed as if the death angels that carried her away were compelled to come back. As I traveled in the spirit, my confidence became greater and greater. Then all of a sudden, her lifeless body swung her left arm around, a faint breath entered her body and I began shaking my head. Wow! When you really press into God, you stop just existing; then miracles and change can happen.

Sarah was taken to Mercy Fitzgerald Hospital, and it seemed like the ambulance was traveling ten miles per hour, no lights and no sirens. Upon her arrival church members started praying. The attending doctor stated that she was in very bad shape and our prayers were futile. Never the less, we wrestled in the spirit and won. Sarah is back, healthy as a horse and it's all because we didn't have a "business as usual attitude," but a "cut me in attitude." The attitude that says, *God, I won't let you go until you bless me*!

One of the most profound stories in scripture that relates to this subject is in the Book of Mark chapter 2:1-12. The story goes like this:

Jesus was in an affluent city named Capernaum. Because of his presence many flocked to see him. Scripture says that there were so many people that the house was filled to capacity. Then came to

Jesus four men standing outside carrying a paralytic and when they couldn't come near the house (watch this) they climbed on the roof carrying the paralytic, tore the roof off the structure, and lowered the paralytic through the roof. Jesus stopped healing everyone else and healed him on the spot.

What was it that caught Jesus' attention? It was the radical, bold, "cut me in" type faith. Could the paralytic be healed if the roof hadn't come off? At some point, but certainly not that day. What drove the men to climb on the roof? They were tired of living life on life's terms and just merely existing. So when it dropped into their spirit that Jesus was in the house, they were not taking "NO" for an answer!

So, the questions for you are:
1. Are you in the house (merely existing) or are you on the roof saying "cut me in."
2. Most important, what are you going to do to get God's attention?
3. Will it be an extraordinary fast, praise, victory over temptation, or will it be a press so hard until God gives up.

The choice is yours…*Cut me in, or cut it out!*

19
THAT ONE MYSTERIOUS SCRIPTURE

My personal assessment of the Bible is **it is** the Word of God, and **the Word of God is truth.** Confirmation for me of this fact is found in Psalms 119:160, *The entirety of your word is Truth*. With that said, there's always a precise chapter, psalm, verse, or proverb that a believer uses for his or her mantra. Notably, Psalm 23 seems to be the most popular. I have adored, trusted and stood on that Psalm as a baby.

Romans 8:11 is a Bible verse I think is somewhat mystical. Now, when I say mystical, please don't associate it with soothsaying, horoscope or some type of divination practice. Here's what it says:

And if the Spirit of the one who raised Jesus from the dead is living in you, then the one who raised the Messiah from the dead will also make your mortal bodies alive by his Spirit who lives in you.

What's so paranormal about it to me is when you feed it into your prayers, spiritually you get a speedy breakthrough. To put it another way, God appears to answer your prayers with breakneck speed. Your response to this might be, "Writer, I have a problem with that because it is the direct antithesis or opposite of what you just taught in chapter 21." And my response would be 'You are 100% accurate.' That's why I said it's a mystery.

Well, the significance of this mystery for me dates back to Resurrection Sunday (aka Easter Sunday) 2010 at my home church, where I am the presiding associate minister. I had the task of sharing the Word of God that Sunday. The prior Sunday, I went on a Men's retreat and attempted to prepare my sermon for Resurrection Sunday. The retreat's resort called Scroon Lake in Upstate New York seemed a relaxing place, with all the trappings to hear from God. For some strange reason, I couldn't get a revelation.

I reconciled within myself that God would come through well before the time I had to speak. The day prior to Resurrection Day I was reading the Bible, conversing with God, and still no revelation. That night, I tossed and turned and suffered great trepidation because at 11:30 AM the next morning, I had to feed God's sheep and I had no food. Then all of a sudden at 9:00 AM, God gave the revelation. Let me share this theology with you. In short, the verse is saying that the same Spirit that raised Christ from the dead, if it dwells in you, is the same spirit that will answer your prayers.

Let's have a Q&A (question & answer) session:

Q) What is the most powerful entity or person known to mankind?
A) God or God's Holy Spirit

Q) How was Jesus raised from the dead?
A) By the Holy Spirit

Q) What other thing in the universe can raise the dead?
A) No power known to mankind.

Q) So, what does the verse mean when it says, "He who raised Christ from the dead will also give life to your mortal bodies,

through His Spirit who dwells in you?
A) What that verse means is that when your spirit is reborn, your other two persons are quickened, or made alive.

Q) Can you give a more exhaustive explanation?
A) Sure will.

God, in the beginning, has always been triune in nature, Father, Son and Holy Spirit. Man is made in the image and likeness of God. Man was created body, soul, and spirit. When man fell from his dominion, so did his three persons. Instead of living in continuous victory, he now lives in sin terminated by death. To that end, he lives in defeat.

Example #1: If the body has cancer, the soul tells the body you will die and the spirit agrees with it because they all speak the same language from sensory perception - smell, taste, touch, hearing, and sight.

However when a man becomes born again, he receives the Spirit of God. What's so different about the Spirit of God? The difference is although the body and soul is not born again, the Spirit is, and the spirit subscribes to a totally different language.

Example #2: When a doctor comes to say to his patient, "Mr. Johnson, by all modern science and statistical probability, because of the stage that your kidney failure is in, we want to put you in a hospice and comfort you because you have one month to live." That's sensory perception, intelligence, common sense that speaks to the body, soul and spirit of a non-believer, and ultimately seals their fate.

Now, adversely, the Holy Spirit doesn't know that language; all it knows is the Word of God. "You will live and not die…" "For with God, nothing will be impossible…" "Come to me…I will show you great and might things in which you do not know." When that is believed, it translates into a quickening of your mortal flesh. *What is a quickening of your mortal flesh?* Your spirit speaks a language of Faith to your circumstances. Once your body and soul hear the language of faith (faith that comes by hearing the word of

God), it brings forth the miracle of what you believed God for, whether it's healing, deliverance, finance, relationship, depression, etc., .

When I taught this on Resurrection Day, God put it to the test in our home worship center and, my God, did miracles manifest! Heart attack victims healed instantly, foreclosures reversed instantly, financial distress healed instantly and the list goes on. This is the way we prayed this scripture:

"Father, by the same Spirit that raised Jesus from the dead is the same Spirit that you will use to answer my petition!"

To date, I've heard scores of testimonies from people who recited that prayer over and over again in their spirit and were answered quickly. I strongly encourage any believer that is facing tribulation to recite this verse, feed your meditation with this scripture and watch your miracle come quickly. I am so certain about this verse that once your breakthrough comes, I want you to email me at lamontmclaurin62@gmail.com so I can post your testimony on my website, http://www.lamontmclaurin.com

20
BUT BY MY SPIRIT

If you've ever examined the way Almighty God brings miracles to pass, notice it's always done by His Spirit. When we look at movies like "The Ten Commandments," we attribute God's miracles to *power, might* and *awe*. Although these adjectives best describe God's ways, they don't illustrate how the miracles are performed. *Remember*, they are performed by His Spirit!

Eight years ago, I was involved in a prison ministry in New York. Through this ministry, God produced miracles. Men from all walks of life, some whom practiced voodoo, Santeria, high priest Satanism, etc. were all converted to the Lord. Broken marriages were put back together, and a great many believers were getting sentence reductions without cooperation from the government.

During that time, I met two Hispanic guys; a Colombian named Nelson Lasso and a Puerto Rican named Jose Caballero. Both men were in their mid fifties, facing possible life sentences. Lasso was tender hearted and just caught up, and was facing a lot of time for heroin trafficking. Jose, on the other hand, was a stout, mean spirited, cut throat red-neck. He was so evil that when he walked, his hand was always fashioned as if to cut or shoot a person. He was indicted for a sting involving six contract murders the government secretly taped and arrested him for before they could happen; he was charged as if they had happened – a fifty year plea with no chance of parole.

During Nelson's incarceration, he joined the ministry; he was naturally repentant. One day after church, I asked Nelson if I could see his indictment and pass it to some attorneys I knew. He responded, "Sure, but I am pretty much finished. My fourth lawyer and the rest all say the same thing - if I got twenty years that would be a miracle!" I said okay but forwarded a copy to my legal team and kept a copy for myself. We met on the issue and concurred with the four other attorneys that Lasso was finished. I spoke with Lasso after church one week later and gave him the bad news. He gave me a glassy eyed stare and responded with a "Kool Aid" smile. "Hey Lamont, have you ever read Zachariah 4:6, *Not by might, nor by power, but by God's Spirit*. I thought to myself, this guy is delusional. I smiled. He responded, "That's the word that the Lord put on my heart. Things are going to happen contrary to what my lawyers and your lawyers think." I responded with a less than candid smile, 'Ok, if the Lord said so!'

I read over Lasso's indictment five more times and concluded that he was by all logical, factual standards, done on both sides and in the middle. Two days before his sentencing, a legal decision "U.S. vs. Shepherd" was passed that affected his initial indictment; he went to sentencing expecting to receive thirty five years. He ended up with sixty months, and is now home preaching the Gospel. The judge himself told Lasso at sentencing that his case was a miracle!

One week later, the news spread throughout the prison and Jose approached me. "Hey minister, what's this sh_t I hear that this Colombian read this Bible verse and now he is getting ready to go home; is that sh_t real?" I said, 'Yep, the judge said so in the transcripts.' He scoffed and said, "That Bible stuff is fairy tale sh_t, this is the real world." I responded, 'Exactly. Believers live in the supernatural realm.'

The next day during a praise and worship service, Jose is standing at a distance, watching. Each day, he gets closer and closer. At the end of the week, he is standing in the group. The following week, he is singing to God. While all of this is going on, I am in awe of God's miracle, praying for his salvation. Later he gets a letter that his wife has cancer. I thought to myself, God, please deliver this man quick; not only is he going to lose faith, but this guy's heart will probably break three times worse.

It's a good thing God is God and I am not. As tribulation began to mount in his life, Jose started to praise God harder, I couldn't believe it, "demon – man" was born again! One day after church, we talked. He said with a big smile on his face, "Hey Lamont, I am really happy." I really have peace in my life, God is so good." I stopped to process his statements and said to myself, "This guy is looking at fifty years, His wife was just diagnosed with cancer, and he says he's happy. Wow, what faith!"

A month passed, and Jose stopped going to legal visits and the law library because he conceded that he would spend his natural life in jail. One day after church I said, 'Jose, let me see that indictment one more time.' He said, "Lamont, it is what it is; don't stress it. I'm good with what's going to happen with me. See, I have joy. Ok, ok! You can amuse yourself." That night I pulled out Jose's legal papers. I saw that he had written Zachariah 4:6 on the front page. I read his paperwork for the tenth time, and saw a mistake that the government made in his career criminal category. Remember I had read this along with seven other attorneys and we never caught this mistake!

The next day I saw Jose and shared the good news. He fell to his knees worshipping God. I wrote the judge explaining the error. At sentencing, he received five years. The judge, an atheist, said to Jose when sentencing him, "Caballero, you are a very wicked man that I was prepared to send away for the rest of your natural life. Although I am an agnostic, this ruling is an act of God; only the Almighty God could have saved you from my wrath." Later, Jose turned to greet his wife; she gave him the news that her cancer was in remission.

Today Jose is a free man and hopefully he is still praising the lord.

Not by Might, nor by Power, but by my Spirit says the Lord of Hosts!

(Zechariah 4:6)

21
DEAD AND STINKING

In the town of Bethany, there was a man named Lazarus, who was near death.

This was the Lazarus whose sisters were named Mary and Martha, the same Mary that anointed Jesus' feet with ointment.

"Therefore his sisters sent for him saying, "Lord the one you love is sick."

When Jesus heard it he said, "This sickness is not unto death but for the glory of God."

(John 11:1-4)

Scripture tells us that when Jesus heard the report, He stayed two more days where He was. Wow, imagine your mother or father sick in a coma with about twenty four hours to live without medical attention! You run to your best friend, telling them to "Come quickly, the one whom you love is sick," and they take two days to come. It gets better. In verse 7 after Christ and the disciples chilled for two days, He said, *Lets go to Judea again.*

Why go to Judea?

If you read the text starting from John, chapter 10:40, you will see that Jesus was beyond the Jordan. Now, Lazarus was dying in the town of Bethany, so geographically the route looked like this:

1. Judea (two days away)
2. Jordan (stayed 2 days)
3. Bethany (Lazarus dying)

Why did Jesus backtrack? Why didn't He go straightway to Bethany? The one and only reason: Jesus wanted to make sure Lazarus was not only dead, but also stinking. Why dead and stinking? Because if Christ would have raised Lazarus from the dead without these properties being manifested, the Jews would have attributed His miracle to some other logic. For this reason, Jesus had to make sure that Lazarus was not only dead, but stinking.

Now, there came a point where Christ was setting the atmosphere to perform the miracle and He asked Martha, *Martha, remove the stone"*... *"But what Martha?"* "But Lord, *by now he has been there for four days and he is now dead and stinking.* Her reply is just like ours today. *But, if and maybe are dangerous words in the Kingdom of God.* Jesus said, (I will take the liberty to do some paraphrasing) *Martha I did not ask you about the biology course you took in Mortuary Science, nor the study that they did on Discovery Channel about cadavers. What I asked you is to remove the stone.* What is that stone today? It is the stone of unbelief. Why did Jesus hold Martha to such a high standard of faith? Not only did Martha and Mary physically witness the miracles of Jesus, but when they anointed His feet, they fulfilled the prophecy in Daniel 9:24 when scripture says, *The most Holy would be anointed.* So, clearly, as a Jew, when she anointed Jesus, she bore witness that Jesus was God in the flesh in John 11:43-45.

Some theologians believe that when Jesus shouted, "Lazarus come forth," the reason He called Lazarus by name is because the whole grave would have resurrected.

Recently, I had a peculiar visit from a childhood friend nicknamed "John." When I answered the door, I said, 'The last thing I heard about you was that you were dead and stinking.' He replied, "I was." I invited him in and without saying anything, we both knew that we were born again Christians. After "chewing the fat" a bit, we exchanged testimonies, and if this testimony doesn't encourage you, then you don't want to be encouraged:

John explained to me that about fifteen years ago he became addicted to alcohol and crack cocaine. His addiction was so voracious that he was put out of every dwelling he lived in because the desire for the drug caused him to steal. Because of his habit, John was relegated to a shelter. He spent so much time in the shelter, that they assigned him a number - #999.

While in the shelter, a staff member whom was filled with the Holy Spirit gave John a Word from God. The word was, "I see your struggle, and I am going to deliver you and show you great and mighty things which you do not know." John was half high at the time, but somehow he embraced the prophecy in his heart. John joined a Bible study at the shelter and they gave him a t-shirt that said *Jesus is a wonder working God*. John used to wear the shirt all the time, even when he went back to his neighborhood to get high.

One day, he went back to his old neighborhood and as he was walking down the street, he heard people shouting, "Hey 999, hey #999". While he was being ridiculed, the crack dealers were laughing hysterically as he approached. One crack dealer said, "Hey triple nine, why don't you bring some of your church members with you next time and I will give you a deal. I know you not the only crack head in the church." John responded, "God is going to deliver me, you watch!" The other dealer said, "Keep dreaming D.S."
John asked, "Why you call me D.S.?" The dealer said, "Because you are dead and stinking." John picked up his package in spite of being mocked, and then headed to the crack house.

As John proceeded to his destination, an eerie feeling came upon him; he said that he felt like he didn't have a soul. Moments later, something miraculous happened. When he began smoking, he began to break out feverishly with hives - so bad that he flagged down a cop to take him to the hospital. At the hospital, he began to contemplate what happened. Ten hours later, John was back at it. He bought crack from another dealer, only to be back in the hospital an hour later.

While in the hospital, John's doctor ran tests and examined him. Final analysis, John was allergic to crack. *Look at God.* Now remember, John had this addiction for fifteen years and never an outbreak or any type of illness, and your garden variety illnesses associated with cocaine use do not include outbreaks of hives.

To make a long story short, John is delivered and set free, because he could not enjoy the addiction, he stopped using. One year later, he got a job working for the Iron Workers Union at $40/hour. The preceding year, he settled a lawsuit for a staggering amount of money. He now lives in a gated community with his wife and grandchildren and drives a new Escalade and a top of the line minivan. Guess what? The numbers in his address are 999. Guess what else? The digits on his license plates to his Escalade are...999. Is it purely coincidence or God's counsel? <u>God's Divine Counsel.</u> This man gave the devil the Word of God in his addiction when the world system said he was dead and stinking; yet he trusted God, and look at him now.

The story doesn't end yet. John has an Outreach ministry and has visited the shelter to encourage the residents. Out of nowhere, he saw the guy who called him dead and stinking. John reached over to the guy, hugged him and began to minister to him. As John began to minister to the man, he noticed the I.D. tag with his name and bed number. Guess what? His number was....999.

The God of the Bible is the God of storms; storms attract God. That is how He shows His awe and power through the storms of your life. But God is also a God of timing. Jesus didn't just jump up and say "Come on disciples, let's run to Bethany; Lazarus needs help now." He said, "Nope, I am going to wait until the perfect time and then I am going to show up and show out." So are the same with John and with you and me! There are times when we just have to reach a point where we are dead and stinking, for God to tell us, "Come forth out of a situation." Lazarus was raised. John was raised and exalted.

22
YOU HAVE WHAT YOU SAY

If you examine the creation account in the Book of Genesis, whenever God created something, He first thought it, and preceded a thought with conversation or a word. You and I were created through a conversation. "Let us make man." In the Book of Mark 11:23, Jesus said, *Whosoever shall __say__ to this mountain, move and be cast into the sea, and does not doubt in his heart, he has what he __says.__*

Through conversation, realities are actualized. Recently, I was at one of my part-time jobs, drug and alcohol therapy. While sitting in a meeting, a client stood up to "share" (to give an inspirational message). He stated his name, and then said one of the most devastating, controversial things that I ever heard in my life. He was 17 years clean and that he was a "grateful recovering addict."

The audience of about 200 people, mostly drug addicts began to cheer and applaud. As this occurred, I stepped out the room to get a soft drink and to process what I just heard. This man had just said he was an addict although he had been clean for 17 years. *To me, anyone who has been clean from an addictive narcotic for 17 years is not an addict but "delivered."* He did not get sick like an addict, he did not steal like an addict, he did not use drugs like an addict, so, therefore, he **was not** an addict. When I began to reason with some of the clients about what the man said, they almost stoned me; they actually defended what he said vehemently. I couldn't prevail against them so I kept the matter to myself.

Two months later, I was at my job working the 11:00 PM -7 AM shift. Before I started, I did a mandatory census count. I toured the entire unit checking <u>everywhere.</u> When I entered the last rooms, guess who I saw in bed? - "The grateful recovering addict." After 17 years of sobriety, good health, healthy relationships etc., he hit rock bottom. Why did he hit rock bottom? This Bible truth:

The power of life and death is in the tongue. As a man thinketh, so is he.

Through this man's subconscious conversations, referring to himself as a "grateful recovering addict" even after 17 years of sobriety, the reality of his words came to fruition. **He had what he said.** He said he was an addict, so the result of his condition was addictive drug use. The Narcotics Anonymous program has a recovery rate of 1 out of 70. The reason most don't recover is because they have what they **say**... "I am an addict"

Four years ago, my Pastor was walking down her street along with a great pastor from New York, Winston Kato, and two members. All of a sudden, she stopped and stared at a bar sitting on a corner. We asked, "Pastor is everything ok?" She replied, "This is my new church." The members and I looked at each other as if to say, "Is she crazy? This is a three story $600,000 building that is definitely not in our budget!" She then looked over and **said,** "I know y'all think I'm crazy, but I need somebody to touch, agree and **speak** a word over this bar; after all, the Bible **says** "You have what you **say**!" Moments later, the pastors from the group believed her vision and prayed with her. The rest of us sat back with smirks on our faces.

One week later my pastor approached the owner of the bar. She introduced herself and then said "Why don't you sell me this bar?" The owner replied, "Ma'am, I don't think you can afford this place and furthermore I am selling it to Koreans for the purpose of selling beer and liquor; and by the way, it needs $250,000 in repairs." My pastor replied, "Here's my number, call me when you're ready." The owner replied, "I told you, it's sold."

Two months passed by and my patient pastor observed a Korean gentleman with construction workers standing outside the bar talking with the owner. She walked up and introduced herself and asked, "Are you the new aspiring owner?" The gentleman replied, "Yes, I am the owner." She welcomed him to the neighborhood and asked about his project. The man replied, "I am planning on making a "Stop & Go" store to sell beer with a second floor Go-Go bar." She replied, "Ok, good luck!" The following Sunday in church, pastor was praying and **said,** "Thank you Lord not only for my new building but also sending men to do the labor that I cannot pay for!" The other member and I still remained skeptical!

Two weeks later the Koreans mysteriously pulled out of the deal after investing $300,000 in renovations. The bar owner approached the pastor and asked, "Do you still want the building?" She replied, "What are you talking about? It was mine all the time!" The building is now my home church where I preside as Associate Pastor, and the only reason it is a church today is because my pastor had a vision, **spoke** her vision, and the vision became a manifestation! The only difference between where she was and where she wanted to be was a **Word.**

*You have what you **say!***

23
IT MUST BE A PONY IN THERE SOMEWHERE

Recently a coworker and I were having a conversation about attitude and how it could chart the course of your life, whether negative or positive. She shared a story with me out of a book entitled *It Must Be a Pony In There Somewhere*. The story goes like this:

There were two men. One was an eternal optimist and the other, an eternal pessimist. One Christmas, they both started wishing, hoping they would be fulfilled. The eternal pessimist said, "I want a room full of gifts. I know I won't receive anything, but I will make the request anyway." The eternal optimist said, "All I want is a pony." When Christmas came and they both ran to their rooms, the eternal pessimist had gifts from wall to wall, floor to ceiling. He responded, "It's about time somebody gave me something." The eternal optimist had a room full of horse manure. Smiling, he began to shovel the manure. After six hours of shoveling, the gift bearers were perplexed, so they asked him why he was smiling. He responded, "It must be a pony in here somewhere!"

In life, you can look at the "proverbial" glass two ways - either it's half empty or it's half full. Believe it or not, attitude is a spirit. It can determine whether you will succeed or fail; your attitude determines your altitude. In the Book of Numbers chapters 13 and 14, God gave a commission to the children of Israel to go and spy out the land. Scripture says that ten men brought back an evil report. They talked about the size of the men in the land, they confessed that they were not able to defeat these men, and they were like grasshoppers in their sight. They were so fearful and pessimistic that they could adopt their enemy's vision (we look like grasshoppers in their sight).

What happened is they never considered who told them to spy out the land and why. All they were concerned with was the negative aspect of the situation, so they inherited the negative. The ten spies never entered into the promises of God, but the faithful, Joshua and Caleb, entered into God's promise. They didn't look at the situation; they looked beyond the situation and entered into the promises of God. When asked about the land, Caleb and Joshua said, "We are well able to take the land."

The Bible recounts a story when Jesus was in Israel comforting a woman that He healed. While He was teaching, someone came to Him to tell Him that an official's daughter from the synagogue was dead. He replied, "Fear not, believe only, and she will be made whole." After He said these bold words, the crowd that gathered laughed Him to scorn, because they knew the girl was dead. Jesus said, "She is not dead, but sleeping."

Right before He was about to perform the miracle of raising the child from the dead, a strange thing happened. He let His twelve or more disciples know the only ones that could accompany Him were Peter, James, John and the child's parents. Why would Christ say such an astonishing thing? There was a reason. The parents were allowed to come in to witness the miracle resurrection. The Bible says by the mouth of two or three witnesses a thing is established. The reason why only three disciples were allowed in was because of their attitudes. When the crowd heckled Jesus about His claim to raise the dead girl, Jesus observed the unbelief in several of his disciples, those He told to stay outside. Why? Because behind every attitude is a spirit. When God performed miracles, it's not by might, nor power, but by His Spirit; so since the spirit of unbelief is a negative spirit, a miracle cannot be produced. Since the spirit of belief is a positive spirit, positive things happen. (Fear not, believe only…).

It was not personal when Christ told the other disciples to wait outside. He knew the end results of the matter were based on belief. Who in your life has to be told, "Wait out here?" If you want to get to the next level, there are just some people that you are going to have to tell, "Wait out here!" Scripture is replete with verses encouraging the believer to be like minded. Your attitude in your thinking could very well chart the course in your life. Right about now you might say, "I believe you on this thought process thing, but I am not sold."

Years before Christ stepped into humanity, there was a man named Job. God described him as blameless and upright; he feared God and hated evil. Job had ten beautiful children he constantly interceded for in prayer. He had a nice house, plenty of money and was basically successful in all areas with not a worry in the world. One day, all in the same day, he lost his wealth, family and health and began a wrestling campaign with God. What really went wrong in Job's life? Did he deceive God? No! Did his children sin? No! Did he have secret sin? No! Scripture is clear, *He was blameless in all his ways.* God would know!

The answer to Job's problems lies in three scriptures:
1. Job 3:25
2. Prov. 23:7
3. Philippians 4:7-8

For the dreaded thing that I feared has happened to me, what caused me to worry has
engulfed me. Job 3:25

Scripture was clear that Job was godly and prosperous. Why all the drama? Proverbs 23:7 says, *For as a man thinketh in his heart, so is he.*

Job actually thought this thing together. He brought all his problems to himself with his thinking. He thought it, and it happened. This is why scripture says "Whatever is true, honest, of good report, noble, pure, think on these things." **Wow!** Job thought on things that he greatly feared that were nowhere in his life and not predictable; intense fearful thinking subsequently caused things to happen to him.

Scripture is clear in Romans 12:2 when it says, *Do not be conformed to the thinking of this world but be transformed by the renewing of your mind.* ("Conformed"-To be with; "transformed"-to cut across or go above.") When dealing with any situation by faith, you never look at the situation, you look past it; you have to look beyond your circumstances and begin to meditate on the God that has sovereignty and control over all situations. This is why you must look at a situation from God's perspective.
Remember, the moral of the story "It Must Be a Pony in There Somewhere?" - The optimist saw horse manure; he knew that horse manure comes from horses, and if there was horse manure present, it must be a pony in there somewhere!

24
WHEN I SEE THE BLOOD

Are you a boxing fan? Ever notice there are just some fighters, whether aggressors or on the defensive, who go ballistic at the sight of blood. I liken that analogy to the God of the Holy Bible. The Jews were in slavery for approximately 430 years, and God promised to deliver them through Moses. There came an occasion when God performed His word. During the Exodus, God wrought great miracles before Pharaoh that caused his heart to be hardened. But when God performed His second to last miracle, during the Passover, it involved blood.

In Exodus 12:1, God prepared Moses for the Passover (this was a foreshadowing of the attributes and coming of Jesus.)

1. Lamb - sacrifice
2. First born - virgin birth
3. No blemishes - sinless
4. Male - Son of God

God told the Jews to kill the lamb and place the lamb's blood on their door posts and the lintels. If you do your homework, the door post and lintels are symbolic of Calvary's cross. God further told Moses in Ex. 12:21-23, *When I see the blood, the destroyer will pass you by.* In like manner, when God sees the blood today he doesn't see you. He 's seen his unique, only begotten Son, Jesus Christ. When you call on the name of Jesus, God the Father doesn't see you, He sees the Blood.

In His Son's blood is your redemption, your justification and all your covenant promises. So yes, you can have His assurance whether Chinese, Spanish, Black, White, Arab, European, African or whatever ethnic background you come from. When you call on God, He doesn't see you. He sees THE BLOOD.

Recently, I received a telephone call from one of my students from my men's recovery class named Sam. When I answered the phone we exchanged greetings, and to my amazement, he was in the hospital near death. I asked, 'What's wrong Sam?' He said, "I can't talk, but my mother is here. She will explain. I am short of breath." I sat up in the bed grieved in spirit while his mother exchanged greetings with me. She said, "Brother Lamont, I am going to get the point. Sam is HIV positive. He hasn't been medicating himself properly. The doctors said "he has no immune system, so by Friday if he's lucky, he's going to die," Those were the bold facts. I am going to get the family together and hopefully your church can take care of the funeral arrangements." Earnestly, I attempted to encourage her by telling her that her son will live again, not knowing that God said her son would live and not die.

We closed the conversation and I told her that I would be at the hospital later, to pay my respects. When I hung up the phone, God spoke to my spirit and it wasn't good for me, but it was good for Sam and his family. In my spirit, God said, "Go down to the hospital and plead My Blood, but you must go forth – believing!" "Speak to his mother and Sam, and tell them, "It Is Written." "Do not speak another word, but "It Is Written" "When the doctor greets you, you tell him "It Is Written" also!

Two hours later I arrived at the hospital. I walked into the room and I anointed the lintels and the doorpost, saying "It Is Written."

Psalms 107:20. After thirty minutes of pleading the Blood, I left. As I was leaving the nurses' station, I overheard the nurses saying disparaging remarks like "Christians are fanatics." I drove home thinking about Sam, and I have to be brutally honest, I began to question whether God told me to say what I said because when I looked at Sam, I thought he was dead then.

A week went by, and I received a call on my cell phone. Sam's name came up. I thought it was his mother delivering me the bad news. I answered and instead of his mother, it was Sam. "What's up Minister Lamont, what's up?" God is good. God is good. God is good." I quickly ushered the conversation past "God is good" because I wanted to know how God performed this miracle. I said, 'What happened?' He replied, "I don't quite know, but my immune system is back in full swing, I feel great and my mom wants to invite you to dinner tonight!" I said, 'Oh my God, Oh my God.' Then I asked when he was coming home. He replied, "I came home yesterday." I never made the dinner appointment, but I saw him at a meeting two days later. Sam looked as if he never had a sick day in his life. There is definitely something about when God sees…THE BLOOD!

25
SILVER AND GOLD I DO NOT HAVE
(THE POWER OF GOD)

Most people who believe in God are always attracted to Him by one or more of his attributes - his holiness, faithfulness, wisdom, etc. Nothing attracts me more than his power!

In Acts 3:1-10, there is a man lame from birth. Never expecting to walk again during his lifetime, he came to the temple to beg. He encountered Jesus and left dancing, praising, leaping, and running. My mind has intractable difficulty perceiving this man's feelings of new hope, new limbs, new opportunities, and etc.

Recently, I was in my church listening to testimonies from the saints and a brother named Greg's witness caught my attention. He informed the congregation that prior to salvation he led a life of revelry, drunkenness, partying and the like - all the while God was calling him to deliverance. God tried to reach him through blessing him with good jobs, monetary miracles, etc. He just could not hear God's voice. One day, he saw an old Vietnam buddy named

Freeman, who was filled with the Holy Spirit. As they exchanged greetings, Greg told Freeman, "I want some of that." Freeman exclaimed, "What?" Greg said, "That thing I see you have." Greg could not discern that Freeman had God's light and His peace on him. So when Greg asked that question, he left God with a dilemma: *all of Greg's life I called him through wisdom. He has had nice cars, girls, and plenty of money. If I give him more, he won't come. I know what I will do. I will call him through tribulation.*

God calls us in two ways:

1. Wisdom first: moneys, cars, reputation, etc.
2. Then if we don't respond, he hits us with tribulation: jail, cancer, broken hearts, etc.

Now it's not God that gives the tribulation, but He grants tribulation permission to hit us to execute destiny. Six months later Greg was drunk coming out of an after hours club and missed a step and fell two flights rendering him paralyzed from the neck down; with an expectancy to live thirty days. As Greg walked through this ordeal, God sent his sisters, Jackie Church and Sarah McLaurin, two awesome women of God, to open up his heart - God was ready to enter. However, as they ministered to Greg, his heart became harder and harder. He began to curse God and indict Him. It was all God's fault! Of course you know God had nothing to do with his use of cocaine, drunkenness and revelry.

One day as Greg was getting closer to the end of his rope he declared, "God if you save me and allow me to walk again, I will serve you all of my life." Moments later, he picked up the Holy Bible (he had once despised) and turned to Romans Chapter 8. As he read God's word aloud his right leg, which was totally paralyzed, jumped and started moving. Then his left leg started to move. He summoned for the doctors both who were atheist and said it was a miracle from God.

Greg is now walking on both legs. He kept his promise to God. He is totally sober, no alcohol, drugs or even cigarettes and not even a craving for any. That's what I call power!

26
WHEN CHRONOS MEETS KAIROS

Human beings are creatures controlled by time. Many are so preoccupied with this fact they wear watches and have digital organizers to keep maximum account of time. Even criminals are asked how much time they received for crimes committed. We ask doctors about the life expectancy for terminal patients. One of the biggest debates for humans is "how does God view time."

In the book of Ecclesiastics in chapter 3:1, the writer says (through divine intervention)"

"To everything there is a season, and a time to every purpose under the heaven."

So clearly God has a dual perspective in which he looks at time because as the writer says, there is a time and there is a season. When God deals with time He deals with the concept of time in two ways:

1. Chronos: an endless quantitative space of time that is on the move

2. Kairos: a space of time in between time that either an event happens, or a passing opportunity that an event happens; and it has to be driven through by force.

If you study the nature and character of God coupled with creation you can conclude that God is a visionary, an architect, a careful planner, and everything he does is absolute.

If you read the Book of Exodus Chapter 5, the children of Israel were dealing with the dilemma of time and condition - something every believer deals with at some point in their walk of faith. To be specific, they complained that ever since they started to walk with and worship God, things had gotten progressively worse and in the eyes of their enemies, they looked liked idiots. They complained to Moses, and Moses complained to God. Moses' response was, "Lord why have you done so much evil to this people and called me to preach your goodness you haven't delivered at all!"

Moses experienced the epitome of spiritual warfare; somewhere in your life you have had the same experience. You prayed and got no answers; you fasted – yet no answers. You have had every pastor and clergyman give you a word with respect to your situation. Some have given you a word of comfort, some were wrong. Some even attempted to be an apologist for God's delay and gave excuses why things haven't manifested - you fornicated six months ago, you missed tithes last February, you gossiped two weeks ago, etc. All of these and more are the wrong answers or dark counsel.

The answer lies in whether your Chronos has met your Kairos. Let's examine a few examples, personal and biblical.

In 1961, my mother Mary McLaurin who already given birth to four beautiful girls, asked God for a boy, with the promise she would dedicate him for the service of the Lord. Well on November 19, 1962, she gave birth to a beautiful nine pound baby boy, me.

Later on in life, a problem arose when she started to question God with respect to my salvation; she became doubtful because she saw herself in Chronos but didn't know God saw her in Kairos. Year-by-year my mother would ask me "Son when are you going to give your life to the Lord?" I would actually make a mockery of the Gospel, but there came a time that Almighty God brought me to my knees by way of three federal indictments. She thought God had failed her all the while God was waiting for Chronos to meet up with Kairos. The same Gospel that I used to laugh at, I now write books about! It took 36 years, but God was faithful to his word.

It's the same with Moses and the children of Israel in the Book of Exodus, chapter 5. They didn't know that they were in their Chronos moment even though God gave them a confirming word in Exodus 6:1, *Now you shall see what I will do to Pharaoh for with a strong hand he put you in bondage and with a powerful hand he will let you go.*

Well in Exodus chapter 15, Moses put words together in a praise song to God, the oldest song on record. *"The Lord has triumphed gloriously. The Lord is my strength, my banner, my salvation. The Lord is a man-of-war."* Why the song? Moses and the rest of the complainers were in their Kairos. The Bible says in Proverbs 13:12 *Hope deferred makes the heart sick* (Chronos) but when the desire comes what you pray for - it is a tree of life (Kairos).

Chronos moments are times when the Almighty builds a relationship with you. It's a time when your faith is tested and when your character is shaped. It is very easy to praise God in your Kairos; actually, it's natural. Matthew 5:46 says, *For if you loved them that love you what rewards do you have? Don't not sinners do the same?* Know who are you during Chronos. Are you an *I will bless the Lord at all times person* or are you a person like Jobs' wife; just curse God and die.

When you can bless God and still be productive in the kingdom of God during Chronos, you are a blessed and complete person. If you only praise God because of condition, you are double minded, unstable in all your ways and shouldn't expect anything but frustration in your prayers. When you master Chronos and walk in the spirit, you will experience complete joy even in the fire.

King David understood that concept well. Psalms 34:1 states, *I will bless the Lord at all times.* Why at all times David? Because David understood that Chronos is always moving and it has to meet up with Kairos.

Nobody understood and taught this better than Christ in Matthew 25:1-12, the parable of the ten virgins in a wedding ceremony. All were first in Chronos:

Then shall the kingdom of heaven be likened unto ten virgins, which took their lamps,
and went forth to meet the bridegroom.
And five of them were wise, and five were foolish.
They that were foolish took their lamps, and took no oil with them:
But the wise took oil in their vessels with their lamps.
While the bridegroom tarried, they all slumbered and slept.
And at midnight there was a cry made, Behold, the bridegroom cometh; go ye out to meet
him.
Then all those virgins arose, and trimmed their lamps.
And the foolish said unto the wise, Give us of your oil; for our lamps are gone out.
But the wise answered, saying, Not so; lest there be not enough for us and you: but go ye
rather to them that sell, and buy for yourselves.
And while they went to buy, the bridegroom came; and they that were ready went in with
him to the marriage: and the door was shut.
Afterward came also the other virgins, saying, Lord, Lord, open to us.
But he answered and said, Verily I say unto you, I know you not.

Fundamentally, Jesus was teaching that God works outside of time, inside of time and in between time.

Time Equals:
- Outside of time = Eternity
- Inside of time = Chronos
- In between time = Kairos

The five wise virgins learned that concept well! The five foolish virgins not only misunderstood the concept but lost out on their Kairos moment. Remember the definition of Kairos is a space of time that an event happens; you must be vigilant enough to drive it through by force if success is to be achieved. So the important question answered is how can you receive your Kairos moment if you stepped out of Chronos? In order for Chronos to meet Kairos you have to be in Chronos (time on the move.) Moving where? Towards Kairos.

Wow!

How You Like Me Now

The Bible says *there is a friend that's closer than a brother*. This is how I characterize my friend, Todd King. He was the first to mention the subject of Chronos and Kairos to me. He has a remarkable testimony, never realized when God thrust him into his Kairos moment.

Precisely eight years today, Todd was going through a very deep situation. He was incarcerated because he refused to cooperate with the government. The love of his life Rashonda, his main supporter, lost hope. This caused Todd to stress out. He lost weight, hair and almost, but for the grace of God, lost his mind.

Todd wrote Rashonda a letter appealing for her to wait six more months for him to return home so they could marry and start a life together. She, in turn, replied that six months was too much TIME to wait. She emphasized the word "time" over twenty times. One month later, she wrote to him and dropped this bomb, "Dear Todd, I had to move on. Time waits for no one." She had met another man that she fell in love with. Needless to say, Todd was completely "torn out the frame." Not only did Rashonda leave him but she leapt into the arms of another man!

As time passed, the Holy Spirit healed Todd's wounds and slowly but surely he accepted the reality that Rashonda moved on. Six months later, Todd was released. Like most former incarcerated inmates, he had to adjust to society; low-budget housing, cheap clothes, low wages, etc. We eventually met and talked about the subject of Chronos and Kairos. Afterwards, he would always say, "I'm in my Chronos groove awaiting Kairos."

Time passed. A friend of mine, Bruce took me house hunting in suburban Pennsylvania to look at model homes. We stopped at a site built on a golf course and I didn't want to go any further. The house reminded me of a quaint size mansion with all the trappings complete with an elevator inside. I said to Bruce, "This is a dream house!"

Eight months later, Todd and I met at the International House of Pancakes to talk business about an overseas venture. Todd mentioned that he moved into a house, but he never told me where. He invited me to his wedding. We later concluded our meeting. I eventually received an invitation to the wedding.

Two months later I drove to his wedding at his new home. The closer I came to his house I remembered looking at dream homes in the area. All of a sudden the GPS said, "You have arrived!" It was the mansion that I had looked at last year. No way! No freaking way! When I walked into the house I went straight to the elevator and there was Todd with a big "Kool-Aid smile' on his face, and a well-deserved one. He was getting married to a Victoria's Secret Model look-alike. He now resided in my dream house. Rashonda, his ex, wasn't present. She texted him and stated that she hoped all went well for him and that she wished that she was his bride.

Let's fast forward to the wedding. After commencements, we ate dinner then the party started. I was standing by a balcony when an old school jam began to play. The name of the record was *How You Like Me Now* by Cool Moe Dee. All of a sudden Todd looked around for me and whispered from a distance "Kairos!"

Wow! What if Rashonda stayed in her Chronos?

27
WHAT YOU WALK AWAY FROM YOU HAVE MASTERED
WHAT YOU CAN'T WALK AWAY FROM HAS MASTERED YOU

Recently I was watching a movie called *Heat* with Robert Deniro, Al Pacino, and Val Kilmer. The movie was about an organized crime group that did random burglaries and bank robberies. What I noticed was that the head of the group had the same principle as the head of the Kingdom of God. The principle was, "You cannot join the group if you cannot walk away from something in 30 seconds." I interpreted that as if there is anything in your life - mother, brother, sister, wife, fiancé, children, etc. that will hinder you from accomplishing the goals of the organization you are not qualified to join.

Jesus said in Mark 8:34, *Whoever desires to come after me, let him deny himself and take up his cross and follow Me."* He says again in another verse, *Anyone who puts his hand to the plow and looks back is not worthy of the Kingdom of God.* What is God attempting to say to the believer? It's simple. *What you walk away from you have mastered, what you can't walk away from has mastered you.*

God said in Gen 1:25 that He gave man dominion over the entire earth. Therefore, the only master you should have in your life is your creator, because He is the only entity that you don't have dominion over. The question for you today is what is it that has dominion over you? What is it that you just cannot walk away from? Is it a drug, a man, a woman, a job, a religion, a church? Is it a home, a neighborhood, a friend, a business?

There is a mystery to walking away from something, and usually it involves motivation from a person or circumstance and most importantly you must have the will to be free. The complicated part about walking away from something is you or an outsider misjudges the power of the stronghold that has you in bondage. For example have you ever heard a mother tell her son or daughter that the person that they are involved with is no good and that they need to leave that person alone? The person in bondage says, "Yes mom" or "Yes dad. You are right and I am going to leave that person alone!" But two days later, if that, they are back in that person's arms. What happened in that scenario? The person misjudged the power of that stronghold and so did the advisor who gave advice from the outside looking in. They told the person what to do, but never told him or her how to do it!

Whenever you cannot leave a thing, you are dealing with "spiritual warfare." Before we attempt to fight the battle, we must understand the mechanics and stages of sin.
1. Sin is appealing
2. Then it is promising
3. Then it is demanding

For example, in the Book of Genesis 38:1-12:
Most theologians interpret the character of Joseph as a just man, and so do I, but I observed a chink in his armor. Joseph was a Hebrew that was sold into slavery in Egypt. God prospered him in Egypt and put him in a prominent position as an officer in Pharaoh's house. But there was a stronghold in the house; it was the officer's wife. The Bible says day by day, he was tempted but never gave into the temptation and that's correct, but he sure didn't attempt to avoid it.

The best weapons to defeat strongholds are these two verses from the Bible:
For though we walk in the flesh, we do not war after the flesh: (II Corinthians 10:3)

And having in a readiness to revenge all disobedience, when your obedience is fulfilled. (II Corinthians 10:6)

Let's break that verse down and let's use two separate scenarios to illustrate the verse:
- Narcotics anonymous, A.K.A. NA uses a cliché in its meetings that contribute to a high percentage of its adherence to be bound in strongholds. The first thing they do in meeting is introduce themselves by name and then say that they are *"A grateful recovering addict."* Now it doesn't matter if they have 20 years clean; this is the destructive cliché that's used.
- Let's look at the lie in this statement. Addict: to habituate or abandon oneself to something compulsively or obsessively. Now if a person goes to a clinic seeking help for the addiction, is the person a grateful recovering addict or is the person in recovery? The person is in recovery if he or she understands the definition, then they can move in the direction of walking away from the narcotic and mastering it because the lie is cast down out of the person's imagination.
- If a person continued to believe the lie that they are an addict, they would continue to function like an addict.
- If a person believed that they are in recovery, a person would function like they are in recovery. Recovery: a return to a normal state of health, mind and strength.

I want to take this time to sort of breakdown verse 4,5, and 6 where it talks about pulling down strong holds, casting down arguments and every high thing that exalt itself against the knowledge of God. Let's examine a few commonalities about most people in bondage over the opposite sex, properties, cars, careers, etc.

- When the enemy comes, because he knows our behavior

(not to be confused with the ability to read our minds) he first captivates you into a stronghold by lying to you.
- His second step is to get you to fantasize about the lie.
- The third step is for you to believe the lie in your mind and turn around and embrace it in your heart. Now you are in bondage and instead of you walking in your God given dominion (authority), you relinquish your authority and now you are a slave.

Example: I recently received a text about a friend of mine who owned a successful car dealership. The text read, "Please pray for our friend. He is in the midst of a life and death storm." Now let's examine what the brother's problem was.

- Obviously he was behind on his bills. He may have been in danger of losing his beautiful home that he cannot afford and his business that's apparently not doing well.
- Clearly he sees his house and business in foreclosure, which normally should have a reasonable emotional effect on a person, but is it a life or death situation?

And the answer is... *Yes* and *No!* Well, how could it be both? If he continues to stress out over an asset that he has no control over, what eventually will happen is he will lose his house, his business and then his life. If he cast down the imagination (replaced the lie with God's truth), then and only then will he have the power to master that situation. It's simple!

- Yes, he may suffer financially if he loses his business
- Yes, he will suffer shame, low self-esteem and the like.
- Yes, he may have to move his family into an apartment.

But will he survive? The answer is yes. Is God able to replace what he lost? The scripture says, *God can do exceedingly and abundantly past what you can think or ask according to the power that works in you.*

What the truth is:
- If God could create this universe, then a home and business is not even a task for him.

What the real concern is:
- How much power do you have to cast down that imagination, stop believing the lie, and stand in God's

truth.

Recently I was listening to the song *How Can I Breathe without You* by Leanne Rhimes. It was well sung and a dynamite recording. There was one problem; if a person were involved in a divorce, separation or break up - it could lead a person to suicide if they listened to it enough. The record started off saying, "How could I breathe without you, how could I live without you." In other words if you died or decided to leave me, I would die and cease to exist. Well as mellifluous as it sounded and as harmonious as the lyrics were it's a lie. While I do think that the general intent was to produce a great love song, *and she did*, at the same time there are scores of people from all walks of life (suffering heartache, depression, suicidal thoughts, etc.,) that could apprehend this lie in their mind (imagination) and then embrace it into their hearts. *Now what he or she can't walk away from has a stronghold on them*. If the lie isn't properly cast down and reasonably dissected you could conclude that:

- You are going to miss that person.
- That person brought a great deal of happiness in your life.
- That person made love to you better than all your past lovers and it's going to hurt.

But is that person the air you breathe?

- Answer: No!

Can you live without him or her?

- Answer: Yes!

How do we know? Because you survived before you met them. Will you ever meet another like them or is it possible to have that joy?

- Answer: Yes! How do we know?

The Bible says in the Book of Genesis 1:28, *be fruitful and multiply*. If God told us to multiply, He must have had a reason and one of the reasons I believe theologically is because when you experience joy through a person, he always has another person set up for you to experience that joy or greater, in the event of death, divorce, separation and the like.

So, you can master every place where your feet have landed! Actually that is your God given assignment, but when we fall in love with the things of the world we become a slave to something and will not be able to walk away.

The Bible says in Deut 6:5 "You shall love the Lord your God with all your heart and strength and soul." Well, why should you do that? *Simple, whatever you have the power to walk away from He has the power to restore. And what you don't have the power to walk away from he can break the mental "chains" and put "bracelets" of peace and freedom around your heart.*

28
ONE HAND WASHES THE OTHER BOTH WASH THE FACE

When Almighty God called Abraham to the faith, He first introduced Himself and then told Abraham to walk upright. It had nothing to do with his posture and everything to do with his lifestyle.

Abraham was an idol worshipper, and the only way an idol worshipper can be converted is through another person endowed with the spirit of the true and living God. So when God told Abraham to walk upright, He essentially was saying, "You must be born again."

When Abraham obeyed God, He reciprocated or returned the favor by blessing Abraham. Thus, the reason why this chapter is entitled "One Hand Washes the Other; Both Wash the Face."

When God makes Himself known to believers, He often does it through covenants. Why covenants? **A covenant is an unbreakable promise sealed by blood.**

Covenants bear witness to the authenticity of God.

Example #1:
Have you ever wondered why the Jews are referred to as God's chosen people? It's simple; not because they are more intelligent, better looking, etc. Far from that! It was to prove the authenticity of God through His promises.

Example #2
In Deuteronomy 28, you will read about blessing and curses. What's so significant about that? They are geared to a certain people, the Jews. If you ever check Biblical or even secular history, you will learn that every time the nation of Israel obeyed or disobeyed these covenants, they were either blessed or cursed.

To that end, God has a system and it's fairly simple:
- Glorify Me. I will in turn bless you. *One hand washes the other, both wash the face!*

Have you ever observed a carnal minded believer, who lives like Lucifer Monday through Saturday, but Sunday becomes Matthew, Mark, Luke and John? They testify that they lay before the Lord, **but** He doesn't answer their prayers. *Why aren't their prayers answered?* God never heard them! Wait a minute! Doesn't God hear all prayer? According to John 9:31, *No!* It clearly says, *Now we know that God does not hear sinners, but if anyone is a worshipper of God, He hears them.*

Wait a minute, aren't we all are sinners? Does that mean God cannot hear us? Yes, He hears you, **but** if you know the Word of God and you know Almighty God and you continue in rebellion, then clearly you hinder communication with Him.

Imagine yourself with a spouse; you both are believers, you know the Word of God, the Spirit of God lives in you, and you are both born again. Just this week you decided to:
1. Abort a child
2. Bear false witness against your neighbor, and
3. Commit credit card fraud.

On Sunday, at church, you hear your pastor recite Mark 11:24, *You have what you say.* Your faith gets charged and you begin to call things that are not as if they were, lay before the Lord, **but** never once stop to forsake the sins you committed against Holy God.

Do you really think God is going to answer your prayers? No! He never heard it. Quite often we testify that God doesn't answer prayer. God clearly says in Joshua 1:8-9,

This book of the law shall not depart out of thy mouth; but thou shalt meditate therein
day and night, that thou mayest observe to do according to all that is written therein: for
then thou shalt make thy way prosperous, and then thou shalt have good success.

I hear you saying, "Well, how can I meditate on the Bible day and night, and then do everything it says? I have two jobs, I'm in school, and have nine kids…" It's very simple.

Example:
In the Book of Proverbs 6:19, God says that it's an abomination to gossip about a person. He hates it. A person from your job says, "Hey, Maria or John, did you hear about what happened to so and so?" Immediately when you respond in the negative, you fall into sin. But if you respond, "Yeah, I did hear about it; can we pray?" Then you have done the will of God.

God reciprocates by activating His covenant and blessing you in a financial, social, material, or spiritual way to demonstrate His good pleasure.

Recently, I was taking a shower and speaking with God about my tithes. I was telling Him that I had something to do with my money that week and I would pay my tithes the following week. What an oxymoron! Immediately, the water turned steaming hot. I jumped out the tub and said, 'Hey Lord, take it easy. I was only playing' (Now it wasn't the Lord that caused my water to malfunction, but I endearingly attributed it to Him). I said, 'Ok, ok! You got it. I will pay my tithes this week as the scripture in

Malachi says:

"Bring all your tithes in the storehouse and try Me now in this, that I will open the windows of heaven and pour out such a blessing that you would not have room enough to receive it.'

Well, I paid my tithes that Sunday. The following Tuesday, I received a phone call and was told a business deal of mine materialized, and a generous amount of money was wired to my bank. I later went to the bank. As the teller put money in the money counter, I stood pondering how I could carry it; I was given ten large envelopes full of money. As I stuffed the money in my sister's pocketbook, I remembered the scripture in Malachi 3:10, *Test me and see if I don't open the windows of heaven and pour out a blessing so that you will not be able to contain it.*

So, in short, John 15:7 will conclude things best,

If you abide in Me and my word abides in you, you will ask whatever you desire and it shall be done for you!)

29
IT AIN'T DAT DEEP!

A worldly phrase commonly used in urban slang is, ***"It ain't that deep!"*** It means that you are putting too much effort, emphasis, or emotion into something that doesn't require a great deal of thought.

I have observed over the past six or seven years sects of members of the local church delve into psychotic behavior. I just bet you are saying, *Wow Lamont, that's a very condescending critique!* I ask you to hear me out, so you will see I say this with respect and love. Sometimes the truth is hard to say, never the less it needs to be stated. Here's what I would like to make known:

I took a close look at the happenings in the local church community. I discovered a very big problem with regard to how church leaders were conveying prosperity, becoming "rich." There was trendy use of scriptures like:

1. "Give, and it shall be given unto you; good measure, pressed down, and shaken together, and running over…" Luke 6:38

2. "Beloved, I wish above all things that thou mayest prosper…" III John 1:2

3. "Wealth and riches are in his house…" Psalms 112:3

"Preachers" were going to great lengths preying on believers' desperation to flee poverty. Thus, schemes were born like "I have a vision that if you sow a $1,000.00 "Millennial Seed" (at least 500 of you) God is going to pour out a financial blessing. Others say they will send you an "anointed" handkerchief to heal financial woes. After talking to scores of church folks, I've come to one conclusion; following such methodologies is foolishness.

It Ain't that Deep!

First of all God never guaranteed in his scripture that **ALL** believers will be rich, or Jesus would not have said in Matthew 28:11, "You will have the poor with you always." The Apostle Paul illustrates the real formula for true contentment in I Timothy 6:6 "…godliness with contentment is great gain."

So minister, what are you saying? Christians just have to wander the earth being poor with no hope? The answer is NO and God forbid! Poverty never glorified God - only contentment with whatever state you find yourself in does. It's not an easy thing. That takes trusting God.

The word of God is true, and He wants you to have his best in heaven and on earth. The psychotic situation that the kingdom has pursued in the most recent past is the wrong method. Jesus says in Mark 11:24, *What things soever you desire, when ye pray, believe that ye receive them, and ye shall have them.*

I attended a church service in January 2013. While testimonies were going forth, a preacher said everyone's financial woes were ended. Hmm! According to what? Ok, so by May when you fall off the fiscal cliff then what? You have to be careful about what you hear!

Here is a secret and it ain't that deep:

God has laws in the earth...Jesus states in Matthew 6:45 *God rains on the just and the unjust."* (Or simply, the saved and unsaved, believers and non believers.)

Let's look at three different types of laws - and what they say.

Spiritual Law
- No one comes to God the Father except through His Son, Jesus Christ

Moral Law:
- If you practice sexual sin, you increase the chances of having poor health (from sexual diseases) or face the risk of death.

Financial Law:
- You have to pay your bills on time.
- You then can have excellent credit.
- If you have first-rate credit, you can go to a financial institution and ask for what amount of money you want. 97% of the time you will get it. With God guiding your' every step, Abracadabra! You are financially on your feet.

No $1000.00 seed offering with broken promises here!

Do these names look familiar to you?
- Walmart
- Remy Hair
- The Gap
- Comcast
- K-Mart
- Apple
- Facebook

Their CEO's are not known to be Bible thumping, religious people, but they have mastered God given laws related to wealth.

There are Christians even today that believe God is like the fictional characters on "Bewitched" or "I Dream of Jeannie." Just make a wish and then sit in a corner and dream about it. Come to church get some "feel good" talk (sermon), get happy and then go back home the same way you came in, just a bit more delusional.

Whenever God blesses someone in the Bible, He always gives them a vision first and then says, "Go get it." God appeared to Abraham in Genesis Chapter 12 and said *I prepared a land that flows with milk and honey, now get away from the land where you are,"* essentially meaning it's not coming to you, you have to go get it. In Numbers the 13th chapter, God tells Moses and the children of Israel the same thing. Moses sent twelve spies to search out the land that God promised, because they had to possess it. The same is true today for the believer. If God makes you a promise, He has already secured the blessing(s); believe God and then take possession of the guarantee.

A few years ago, a female testified in a church that she prayed to God to bless her finances and nothing happened. I later found out she was not employed) She cried, hollered, and eventually she fell to her knees. The pastor attempted to comfort her by saying, "God didn't forget you, it's just not your season." I noticed that her testimony cast doubt on some in attendance.

After the service, I spoke to this woman and asked her some pointed questions.
1. 'What was your major in college?' She responded, "Human Services.
2. 'What's the highest degree you have?' She said, "A Masters degree."
3. 'Have you been on any employment websites that advertise Human Services positions?' She said, "Not recently."
4. 'Do you have credit cards?' She responded, "They are all burned out."

I allowed her to share as much personal information as she chose, eventually ending the conversation. While walking away, I observed to myself, *Wow, this woman has the potential to earn up to 100,000 a year. Get a job pay off your cards, the game changes.* The deep part is that she had shared she spent a minimum of 14 hours a day on social media. *Wow, not one hour on the computer searching for careers,* but you come to church blaming God. *Wow!*

Take a look at this comparison:

- A drug dealer walks in unrighteousness. If he is in business for at least 3 months successfully, sells a decent product at a good price, he becomes financially successful.
- The typical believer you find in church today may have been serving God a considerable time, walks in righteousness, has the covenant of God's Word, BUT is broke and in financial turmoil.

This really is sad but true!

God said in his word in Romans 14:17 *That life with God is joy and peace in the Holy Ghost*; it does not say stressing about finances is a part of Gods plan.

In a capitalistic society like America where financial opportunity is abundant, there is no reason why Christians are walking into worship broke and defeated with frowns on their faces; non believers are walking around with smiles on their faces with a pocket full of money.

Let's review what you need to do:

- Pay your bills - Roman 13:8 *Owe no one anything but to love them.*

- Receive the vision - Proverb 29:18 *Where there is no vision the people perish.*

- Go Get it - Deuteronomy 8:18 *And you shall remember the lord your God for it is he who gives you power to get wealth.*

- Don't sit back dreaming, Ecclesiastes 11:4 *He who observes the wind will not sow, and he who observes the cloud will not reap.*

GO GET IT, It's not that deep!

Last, but not least...Tithes.

So you're saying, "Wow that's great so I don't need to pay my tithes!" NO, actually it's crucial that you pay your tithes to keep covenant with God. The Prophet Malachi said in Malachi 4:8, *Will a man rob God, in tithes and offering?* Failure to pay tithes is tantamount to robbing God. King David thanked God for the very privilege of being able to give to the work of the Lord:

"But who am I and who are my people that we should be able to give so generously. Everything comes from you and what we give to you comes from your hand."
(I Chronicles 29:14)

Tithing has long been a mystery to the kingdom but in Deuteronomy 26:12 God makes His purpose clear - it is for the pastor, the homeless person, the children with no father, and the single women who are struggling with their kids. To that end God has already given you vision. Ask Him for favor with respects to world news, jobs, or financial instruments that will put you in a position to receive funds to jump start your dream; THEN go get it!

Keep in mind "He who observes the wind will not sow, and he who observes the cloud will not reap"

It's not that deep!

30
DON'T THINK IT STRANGE

When you pray and believe God for a miracle expect the adversary to attempt to cause you to disbelieve the word of God! In the Book of I Peter 6:7, God first tells us how precious our faith is, and then begins to tell us what purifying agent He is going to test our faith with. Then he warns us a final time in verse 12 *Not to think it strange when that fiery trial comes to try us as if something strange has happened to us.*

Have you ever prayed on a matter and things progressively worsened and you turned around and doubted God? Why doubt Him if he warned you not to think it strange when you pray and things get worse? It's tantamount to walking up to an occupied property and reading a sign that says, "Beware vicious attack dogs are on the premises" in neon lights. You think about what it says, and proceed to enter the premises. Upon entering the premises, you get attacked by three 150 pound Rottweiler's, end up with 75 stitches, and turn around and say, "I don't know why these people let those wild dogs run loose!"

In like manner, God has given us a clear warning and also promised to deliver us from the fiery trial.

Exactly what is a fiery trial? Let's first look at the adjective "fiery."

The Greek word here describes an intense fire that burns away impurities. But I believe God is speaking more exhaustively than that. When you begin to trust God through faith, you must first understand what faith means:

Now faith is the substance of things hoped for, the evidence of things not seen. (Hebrews chapter 11:1)

The operative words in that verse are **hoped for** and **not seen**. One of the devil's greatest tricks is your five senses: sight, smell, taste, touch, hearing and most of all your eyes. This is his favorite list. Take a look at the fall of man:

In Genesis 3:1-6, with no introduction the serpent appears on the scene in paradise. The first thing the serpent does is to cause Eve to question the Word of God but before that that slick rascal did something very subtle. He didn't call God by his right name Yahweh Adonia (Lord God). He just called Him God. The serpent's second step was to boldly deny the truth of God, in essence calling God a liar. The serpent's third step was to appeal to Eve's senses "You will be like God!" God's fullness of knowledge was only one of the superiorities that set him apart from humans. But the serpent combines all of God's superiority over the woman into this one audacious appeal.

Now when the serpent got Eve distracted through mind games he knocked her clean out with the eye game. When the woman saw that the tree was good for food, that it was pleasant to the eyes, and a tree desirable to make one wise, she took an ate of it. She also gave it to her husband and he ate.

Eve was completely torn out the frame. The serpent had her so open until she forgot the simple remedy to his deception, "Hey serpent why don't you eat first and if it works, I will try it." No! She fell hook line and sinker; the very same way you and I will fall if we are not vigilant and sober.

How do you protect yourself against satanic oppression?

First, you must know who the devil is and his characteristics. One of the greatest deceptions Hollywood has done is to make Satan, the devil look like Freddy Kruger, Jason from *Friday the 13th* or the Boogie Man. It's all a fairytale; the devil is a spirit and as Jesus said in Luke 24:39, *A spirit doesn't have flesh and bones as you see I have.*

The devil cannot bite you, make you levitate, or impregnate you, but one thing he does well; he speaks into the ear of our mind and causes us to lie, cheat, steal and doubt God. We can't quite explain how he does it, but we know that such mind to mind communication takes place.

Most Christians cannot discern between demonic activity and life challenges. I once met a believer whose car wouldn't start and he was late for Bible Study; he attributed the car not starting to Satan's providence but after careful investigation we found out that the battery post connectors were corroded with acid; thus the car wouldn't start. If he had kept up with his car's maintenance, he wouldn't have had the problem.

I met another young believer who told me that her husband had a sexual demon in him that he needed cast out. This woman was a very attractive woman with a very good career. I asked what made her think her husband was possessed. She responded because he wouldn't stop having affairs with other women. At that point, I discerned that the woman wasn't holding the husband to a biblical standard, and he was just having his cake and eating it too!

I counseled the couple and advised the wife to ask for a separation with reconciliation in mind. During the separation, I told the wife to keep him guessing. The reason I instructed her in this manner is when a counselor instructs a woman to live holy and obedient before her husband, the husband learns to despise her; when the husband is kept guessing, then the tribulation can have its perfect work. (I learned this studying marriage counseling.) Her schedule started to change. She dropped a couple of pounds, changed her hairstyle, yet all the while, she remained virtuous. When her husband thought that maybe his wife was playing the same game that he freely played for years, this mysterious "demon" was cast out. The couple got back together stronger than before. What happened to the sexual demon? It never existed. It was the tribulation that caused the husband to stop his adulteress activities and to love and appreciate his wife like Christ loved the church.

So what is demonic oppression?

You prayed for something, it hasn't manifested and now you doubt the truth of God - that is satanic oppression. It can happen in the most mature believer.

Let's examine two primary ways that Satan oppresses you. Listed below are his favorites:

1. Doubting
2. Temptation

Let's deal with doubting first. I cannot think of a better chapter than with Matthew 4:1-12.

After reading this chapter, some may say it appears that Satan was tempting Jesus and they would be right, but his ostensible purpose was to attempt to get Christ to doubt God. You see when Christ came to this earth, He had two natures.

100% Man and 100% God

So, when Satan came to Jesus, he didn't come as a physical demon; he came as a spirit. So what Jesus was going through was not a physical battle, but a battle that you and I deal with daily; a battle in the mind. I was always taught that Satan has a physical nature in Matthew 4, and Luke 4. Jesus was alone in these chapters dealing with a mind battle. And I am willing to prove it. Let's examine the scriptures.

When you read Matthew 4:1-3 it tells a story as if Jesus encountered a physical demon, but when you read Luke 4:3 (which is more investigative) *and the devil said to him.* **Where did the devil come from? When did he enter the picture?** He was always in the picture, but not physically. He dealt with Jesus the same way he deals with you and me every day. He started talking to his mind while he was in the wilderness.

What is the wilderness, a broken marriage, financial challenges, unemployment, addiction, scandal, homelessness, disobedient children, failure?

No, this wilderness isn't something you see on Discovery Channel; this is a battle for the mind.

Question, who won the battle between Jesus and Satan? **It was Jesus**! Did Jesus say Satan I rebuke you in the name of Jehovah? Did Jesus use some secular saying like *God don't like ugly*? No! Far from that! **Jesus did the two most powerful things you can do in a spiritual battle.**

1. He never fantasized about the temptation
2. He gave Satan the word of God

So, why can't I just rebuke the devil?
- Because when you rebuke the devil the lie never goes away

Example:
Have you ever been in the will of God and been tempted by the devil, overcame the temptation by rebuking the tempter or just said no; but then fantasized over the temptation anyway until the next trip and it socked you out of the box back into adultery, back into addiction, back into scandal and or back into lawlessness? If that was you, just give me a little grin.

Well, why were you defeated? You rebuked the devil didn't you?
- Yes, you rebuked the devil but you made a huge mistake. You never replaced God's truth with Satan's lie. *At all times, Jesus replaced his lie with God's truth; then and only then does the fantasy leave your mind.*

The second manner of oppression is temptation.

One of my most favorite characters in scripture is a holy man by the name of Joseph. Joseph was a slave in Egypt who rose to the rank of Vice President. There was a point in the story where Joseph was living in the household of the Pharaoh's captain, Potiphar. Potiphar's wife cast longing eyes on Joseph. Day by day, she would appeal to Joseph to sleep with her. Now this was not your average temptation, because we have to assume that Joseph was living a life of celibacy, and the women of that date in Egypt were extraordinarily beautiful.

Most women of status spent a great portion of their time engaging in beautification. So we have to imagine that Potiphar's wife was extremely attractive. Scripture says that she was so desperate for Joseph that she caught him by his garment and said, "Come have sex with me!" How did Joseph respond? He ran. Why did he run? Why didn't he just rebuke her in the name of Yahweh? Simply because the temptation was so overwhelming that Joseph would have sinned if he stood there to negotiate with her. You didn't think that Joseph wanted to have sex with this woman? I believe he wanted her as bad as she wanted him, but his primary objective was not to sin against God. Certainly committing adultery with this woman would have been a sin, so he ran.

The Bible says to flee youthful lust. Why run? Because when you run, it gives you the ability to resist the temptation better. Often men like to play the game "Pity Pat" with the devil, especially Christians. I often hear men and women who were once held in sin's bondage tell testimonies of how they went to different places to preach the gospel. Places like bars, parties, old neighborhoods, old acquaintances, and in its appearance, it seems like they were evangelizing but often we're playing "Pity Pat" with the devil.

Don't agree? Think I am being judgmental? Didn't Jesus say, *Go into the all the world and preach the gospel?* Yes, the Lord did say that but he also said, *be wise as a serpent and innocent as a dove.* Do you think that it is wise for a saved ex-degenerate gambler who lost his family, job and home to dine in Atlantic City because he is now saved? Or should a saved, sanctified, Holy Spirit filled person who was once addicted to alcohol have a glass of wine with dinner maybe once a week? These are just a couple of examples of playing "Pity Pat" with the devil.

God's word clearly instructs us to run from temptation...not walk to it. There are times when you can become so religious that you deceive yourself of who you really are. You think you are delivered, but you are actually transitioning into your new birth.

Have you ever had the occasion of sitting in church during testimony time and listening to the testimonies that come forward?
- "I thank and praise God that he delivered me from this…
- "I bless God's name because I overcame that…"

And then bang, all of a sudden the very thing you confessed you had dominion over now has you in bondage. Why does it have you in bondage? **Because, at times, you can deceive yourself that you have dominion, when all the while it's God's grace that has stabilized you;** but its deception has you thinking that you can play "Pity Pat." **It's that same deception that will place you back in bondage!**

Don't think it strange!

Beloved, think it not strange concerning the fiery trial which is to try you, as though some strange thing happened unto you. (1Peter 4:12)

31
THE HICKEY DOO

Recently, one of my students was caught cutting a class. As Carlton Clark, a disciplinary staff member, explained the scenario to the principal, he used a street term called the "hickey doo." I grinned. The "hickey doo" is a term used by con men after they have duped an unsuspecting victim. Clearly, the student's story was that they were in one place, when actually they were in another place (they attempted to dupe the staff into thinking they were innocent, when in actuality they were not.)

One of the greatest and most harmful tricks that the devil uses is an acronym called F.E.A.R. False Evidence Appearing Real. Although the evidence is false, dang does it seem real!

Have you ever had the experience of walking in the will of God, I mean on point with your love life, your obedience, your sanctification, etc. You turn around, and the sinner (on your job, next door neighbor, relative, etc.) appears to be prospering more than you? I coin that as the "Hickey Doo."

The "Hickey Doo" is a maneuver that the devil uses to rob, kill and destroy your faith. How he does it is what I call a three step drop.

The reason I coin it as a three step drop is if you don't stand after the three steps outlined below you will most certainly get dropped.

The first step is to get you to look at your condition. (Distraction)

The second step is to get you to look at the Word of God. Verse like Deut. 28:13, Eph. 3:20, Jer 33:3, Ps 1:3 which promise you victory in your condition.

Step three is after you complete step one and two. You have examined your condition your condition is bad. You are holding on believing God. You have fed your prayers scripture; you are optimistic about what God is going to do and then all of a sudden the Hickey Doo. The person who curses like a drunken sailor, commits crimes, adulterates, lies, steals, fornicates, etc., gets a new house, new car, and Uncle Johnny left them $100,000 in a CD in his will.

If you are not wearing the full armor of God, this is enough to get you to walk clean out of faith. About 2600 years ago a holy man of God, Habbakuk, was experiencing the "Hickey Doo." The Book of Habakkuk is a precious book, because it opened up with a complaint and closed with praise. This book opens with Habakkuk asking God "How long shall I cry and you will not hear?" It seemed to him that God was allowing the wicked to prosper but did nothing to straighten out the condition of the righteous. (Hickey Doo)

But watch how God responded to Habakkuk's complaint in verse 5:

I will work a work in your day, which ye will not believe, although you were told.

In Habakkuk chapter 2, God told the prophet to "Write the vision down and make it plain on tablets, that he may run who reads it, for the vision is yet or an appointed time, but at the end it will speak, and it will not lie."

An appointed times speaks of a determined time in God's

judgment, delay doesn't mean denied. God knows his plan and it work according to his purpose. The righteous are supposed to study and proclaim His Word while waiting on the fulfillment.

What's telling is God must have moved in Habakkuk life in a victorious way because the complaint turned into praise:

Though the fig tree may not blossom nor fruit be on the vine.

Through the labor of the olive may fail. And the fields yield no food. Though the flock may be cut off from the fold. And there be no herd in the stalls. Yet I will rejoice in the lord I will joy in the Good of My salvation the lord is my strength.

He will make my feet like deer's feet. And He will make me to walk on high hills.

(Habakkuk 3:17-19)

Habakkuk understood the mystery of deflecting the Hickey Doo. Although things are not good now, in God's perfect time, He is going to absolutely blow me up. Have you ever watched a deer climb a mountain? They do it with supreme confidence. He will make my feet like deer's feet.

Well, how about the unrighteous? I still had to suffer while serving God and he was blessed and never suffered? Knock, Knock! Who's there? Hickey Doo. He's back.

Let's examine the mystery why God allowed the wicked to prosper.

Psalms 37:1-3:

Do not fret because of evil doers, nor be envious of the worker of iniquity. (1).

For they soon shall be cut down like the grass, and wither as the herb. (2).

The Lord laughs at him because he sees his day coming. (3).

About two years ago, I was suffering from a serious case of Hickey Doo Syndrome, and boy did I have it bad! I was serving in my prison ministry, which encompasses ten different institutions, I taught at five different Bible studies, I attended church five days a week, fed the homeless, practiced celibacy, researched material to write this book and others. I mean I gave Matthew 6:33 some substance. Then came a day that I was leaving out the door to go teach at my church's Bible Study, and I found that my vehicle was on empty and I had two dollars to my name.

While sitting in my car pondering my condition, an old acquaintance rode by in an S-600 Mercedes 2012 Edition and said "Are you still in that church foolishness?" I replied 'Yes, it's that foolishness that sustains me.' He shrugged his shoulders proudly as he looked down on me and sped off.

I sat there for approximately thirty minutes and had a serious discussion with God. I said 'God what part of the game is this? I am walking by faith, honoring your name, proclaiming your Son and broke. This heathen don't fear, honor or reverence you! He just called your Son a fool and he is in an S-600; all I ask for is a little gas money to preach your word!' As I concluded my discourse with God, He answered me instantly. His first response was "My Grace is sufficient, for when you are weak, then I am made strong!" That set me straight.

Then God in almost an audible tone started to explain the mystery of the righteous and unrighteous:

He said, "Lamont, how long is the average man's life?

I responded, 'About 60 to 70 years.'

He said "How long is eternal life?

I responded, 'Forever.'

He responded "Am I a fair God?"

I responded, 'Absolutely.'

He responded, "Okay, if that person in the Mercedes lives to be seventy years old and never accepts my Son as Lord and Savior, he just condemned himself to hell without ever experiencing the exhilarating eternal Joy of Heaven. You, on the other hand, if you died right this very second, would leave this dimension of time and translate straight into eternity, never to experience heartache, pain, disease, or death. Because I am sovereign, is it not fair that I allow the wicked to have their heaven on earth, because they will never experience the next dimension, Heaven."

I replied, 'Wow, Wow, and Wow Wee!'

While I was exasperating my wows, He said, "Imagine you at a birthday party in Heaven. You have all your family with you and they are singing you a birthday song "How old are you now, how old are you…" and you reply "I am a zillion years old. Would you really look back at that person in the S-600 Mercedes who called my Son a fool with envy or compassion?"
I answered, 'Compassion, much, much compassion. Thanks Lord for the revelation.'

And ye have forgotten the exhortation which speaketh unto you as unto children, My son, despise not thou the chastening of the Lord, nor faint when thou art rebuked of him:

For whom the Lord loveth he chasteneth, and scourgeth every son whom he receiveth.

(Hebrews 12:5, 6)

32
LORD I BELIEVE BUT HELP MY UNBELIEF

Mark 9:23-24

My favorite Bible text is about the man who comes to Jesus with his demon possessed son, hoping that the boy would be healed. Jesus says to the man, "All things are possible to those who believe."

Listen to the powerful response of the man. He says, "I believe, but would you help my unbelief."

So the question at bar is can faith and doubt co-exist? I know my theology will be greatly challenged, but the answer is a resounding YES.

Have you ever met a person with what's called a true believer mentality? Always glassy eyed, excited, smiling brightly and doesn't have a doubt in this world. Believe it or not, their faith is an unhealthy faith.

If you read the scripture, Jesus never rebuked the man, but helped his unbelief. A faith that is challenged by adversity, some tough questions or in trepidation is often a stronger faith in the end. 1 Peter 1:7 says *your faith will be tested by pure fire*. So while it seems healthy to always think wonderfully and everything is great, what happens to that person when God says NO? Usually something catastrophic. The question is can that faith pass the NO?

So faith at its tap root is a decision of will. At the end of the day when the rubber meets the road and you scratch below the surface, either there is will to believe or a will not to believe. That is the core of it; the decision to believe or not to believe.

If you ever read John 12:37, the Bible elaborates on a story and then says, that even after Jesus had done all these miraculous signs in their presence, they still would not believe in Him. Then two verses down it says, *"for this reason they could not believe."*

Approximately 25 years ago, I worked at a group home for troubled youths. I met these two young ladies named Stephanie and Sarah. They were biological sisters, had the same D.N.A., the same life challenges, but had two different results with respect to careers.

Let's examine Stephanie's lifestyle. Today, Stephanie is approximately 44 years old. She has 13 children and is addicted to crack cocaine. Sarah on the other hand has one child. She has a dual master's degree. She recently earned another degree that allows her to be a school principal. Her earning capacity is approximately $200,000 per year and she lives adjacent to one of the richest townships in United States, which is Lower Merion.

Question, how could two siblings with the same life experiences, end up with two totally different results. Was it luck, fortune, favor or was it will?

The answer, it was human will on behalf of both sisters'. Although Stephanies lifestyle is looked at in the negative, she willed herself to be a crack addicted mother of 13. Conversely, her sister Sarah with the exact same family willed herself to be delivered from the impoverished institution lifestyle that was presented from her youth. One used ther circumstances as a crutch, the other as a catalyst and when the wills were set in motions, the results were manifested.

It may appear that I am being judgmental against Stephanie but I am not. What I am attempting to do as practically as possible is to draw a distinction between why people fail and why they succeed. It's not always circumstances, but human will.

What do you want? What are you willing to sacrifice for it? How bad do you want it?

Last year, I was watching a show called NFL Network with its host, Deion Sanders. Deion was interviewing the football commissioner, Roger Goodell, about the alarming rate of African American football players that were constantly having run-ins with law enforcement and their use of drugs. When asked the question why do African Americans have the propensity to continually practice lawlessness and use narcotics. Deion Sanders suggested that it was because of lack of family structure and that if the father was prevalent in the African American home, we wouldn't have this problem of African American Athletes running into problems with the law and ramped drugs use. Roger Goodell then objectively agreed with him, or put in another way, gave African American athletes a huge crutch to lean on.

If you were committed to truth, you would have to agree with me that Deion Sanders and the commissioner were clueless when presenting their opinion on the problems, at its taproot again it's a matter of will.

Football may be one of the most competitive, challenging sports on the face of the earth. To become a professional football player a person must have great intestinal fortitude (or human will). The money is unbelievable, so not only is the human will at an optimal level, the catalyst is the money to continually motivate the player to stay focused or will themselves into their destiny.

So when an African American football player who makes 4 or 5 million dollars a year as opposed to $25,000 per year decides to carry guns illegally, sell drugs illegally, take drugs illegally, and the like, it has absolutely nothing to do with family structure; it has everything to do with will. You either have a will to succeed or a will to fail.

In the Book of Genesis, Almighty God wrestled with a man named Jacob, all night and guess who lost? Almighty God! You may say, "Wait a minute author you got to be kidding!" This goes against the omnipotence of God and in actuality it doesn't. It just serves to show mankind when he wills his faith just how awesome he can be.

33
FAITH TO KILL FOR

Recently I was engaged in a conversation with a caller on my talk show *Reason for Hope* on WNAP 1110 AM. The caller, Linda Coleman, wanted to talk about a couple that was recently arrested for the death of their second child due to their belief in faith healing. Linda was very knowledgeable of the scriptures and gave a very revelatory spin on faith healing that has been misunderstood for years in the church. Linda led the audience to scripture in Luke 10:30, where a man was robbed and fell among thieves and the Good Samaritan went to him, bandaged his wounds, poured oil and wine on him, and took care of him. Wow Jesus the Christ, the living Word of God essentially saids "Go get medical attention."

The reason I coined this chapter *Faith to Kill For* is essentially because the couple was taught wrong, they apprehended wrong teaching in their minds, then embraced it into their heart, which subsequently led to both their children dying. They actually lived out what they believed. Not only do they have to live with the horror of having two dead children - deaths they are held directly responsible for, but they have two other pressing matters they have to live with day to day for the rest of their natural lives.

1. The prospect of 25 years behind bars.
2. The thought of thinking that God lied to them.

While I have no authority in the first matter, I am addressing the latter matter because scripture is clear in Number 23:19, *God is not a man that he should lie, nor a son of man, that he should repent, has he said it, and will he not do it, or has he spoken, and will he not make it good."*

Let's compare this to Isaiah 53:5 the end result on the matter of faith:

But he was wounded for our transgressions (sins). He was bruised for iniquities (sins). The chastisement for our peace was upon him, and by its stripes we were healed.

This verse is one of the most popular of verses in Christian circles that is repeated endlessly when the subject of healing pops up. However these words from Isaiah 53:5 have been grossly misunderstood the focus is not on <u>physical</u> healing but rather on <u>spiritual</u> healing.

Let's examine my theory in light of the scripture.

Q) Who was Isaiah speaking about in this scripture?
A) Jesus

Q) When Jesus was crucified, what was the purpose of his crucifixion?
A) To die for the sins of the world

Q) Was Jesus beaten?
A) Yes, according to the scripture.

Q) So what does "By his stripes we are healed" mean?
A) It means what it says, the purpose of his coming and his atonement on the cross was to pay for the world's sin not to guarantee that you will never get sick and in the event of sickness you need not seek medical attention. That thinking is foreign to the text.

Let's look at Numbers 23:19:

1) It's an immutable fact that God cannot lie because He can do everything. He doesn't have a motive to lie. Every lie requires a motive.
2) Has He said it, and will not do it. The question at bar is did God say it?

If this couple was committed to truth they would have to admit that Isaiah 53:5 refers to spiritual healing not physical healing and that God never instructed them to watch two children suffer and die! While their faith was admirable their discernment stretched credulity to the breaking point. Never the less I offer my fervent prayer for their healing and recovery of their spiritual sight.

Q) So what are you saying? God cannot heal?
A) God forbid. I watched and experienced too many miracles to say that He doesn't heal today. What I am attempting to illustrate is that the healing is not guaranteed. We will all die; the rate is one per person. Additionally, I marvel over God's intervention to heal cancer, AIDS, congestive heart failure, etc., but I believe the bigger miracle is the manner and complexity that he has wired us.

Example 1: How does a person know when he may be experiencing kidney failure? He has what's called symptoms, change in color of urine, dizziness, soreness in the area.

God has wired us so uniquely and wonderfully that our organs have sensors programmed in them to tell us to go get help when they malfunction. Turning away from this specific incident and getting back to the subject of killer faith, let's get back to Numbers 23:19 specifically, *Has he said it, and will he not do, or has he spoken, and will he not make it good.* Millions of souls in the kingdom of God are suffering from delusion, mental health (bipolar) anxiety because of this issue. They <u>believe</u> what they want to believe or believe what someone told them to believe without first involving the one (God) who they supposedly put their trust in for the manifestation of the object.

Example 2: I was talking to a female friend of mine and she shared with me that she was in love with a man that she was having an adulterous affair with and (watch this,) the Lord told her that the adulterous man is going to be her husband, and God is not a liar. As laughable as this story is, I can't just pawn the story off as a believer who misunderstood the scriptures. It's much more serious than that. She heard from a spirit and turned around and <u>believed</u> the spirit and identified that spirit as God. That is serious business. Why? Because of her belief, that is her <u>reality</u>. There is a difference between truth and reality.

Reality: Anything you believe to be true.
Truth: Is a core <u>set of facts</u> that are consistent with reality or that is provable

The truth of the matter is biblically God encourages marriage, discourages adultery and hates divorce. God has given the believer something called wisdom, and he describes in Proverbs 3:13-18 that wisdom makes a man happy, and prosperous, and that all her ways are pleasant.

Because the woman thought with her passion and emotions instead of wisdom, she actually believed God spoke to her about breaking up a family, so she could then covet a woman's husband. When attempting to hear from God to understand a vision or a revelation, God speaks to us by the Holy Spirit through his Word.

Example:

Jesus said in Matthew 7:21 one of the wisest but simplest sayings in history of the world; *You shall know a tree by the fruit it bears.*

If the woman wanted to know if she heard from God or Satan she could have read Galatians 5:19:22, where it gives the character and voice of God, and the character and voice of the devil; or the fruits of both spirits.

Galations 5:19: Now the fruits of the flesh are clear fornication, adultery dissentions, hatred, jealousy, envy and the like.

Galations 5:22: But the fruit of the spirit is love, joy, peace, patience and self-

control.

So the question is which spirit did she listen to? It was a satanic spirit, because her actions involved the fruits of his character. To know you heard from God or that God is speaking to you, his word must harmonize with his character and your petition.
Often pastors, in error, prophecy false visions to believers whom subsequently embrace them in their heart; the believer is then off to the races.

Example 3: A single woman is looking for a husband. A man walks into the church; he has no ring on to say he is married. He is tall, nice looking and personable. The single woman then observes that a good looking single man has just walked into the church, and she is admiring him. The pastor then meets with the single woman after church and then says, "The Lord told me that the single man is your husband."

What's wrong with that picture? Did God speak or common sense? Did the pastor truly hear from the Lord or was the pastor overtaken by fulfilling the woman's prayer and then magically heard from God? What is the danger in that scenario? Suppose the single man came there because another woman invited him and she was late for service that day?

How does the pastor explain the revelation away? Additionally what happens to the believer's faith; does it get stronger or does disbelief set in?

Scores of believers suffer from "faith" that kills. Mainly because they don't read scripture for all it's worth, nor do they test what is being told to them. I am very skeptical of a pastor that God speaks to every five minutes. The Lord said you are going to find a husband; the Lord said you are going to be rich; the Lord said you are going to get a new home. As kind, loving, and sincere as that pastor might be, the problem with that methodology is, it never came from the mouth of God, and scripture is clear in Proverbs 13:12: *Hope deferred makes the heart sick, but when desire comes it is a tree of life.* Now if deferred hope makes the heart sick (depressed, disappointed, anxious, uneasy), what happens when the desire that's supposed to come never comes? If that desire is a tree of life, then that false hope is the opposite which is death.

It is crucial, central, germane, axiomatic that not only you search the scriptures to understand what God is saying to you, but also test your leaders because scripture is clear in Deut 18:22: *If a prophet or a person speaks something in the name of the Lord and that thing doesn't come to pass, that prophet or that person flat out lied to you.*

He who has ears let him hear what the spirit says to the believer.

34
RUNNING WHILE YET STILL DARK

The first day of the week cometh Mary Magdalene early, when it was yet still dark unto the sepulchre, and seeth the stone taken away from the sepulchre.

Then she runneth and cometh to Simon Peter and to the other disciple whom Jesus loved, and saith unto them, they have taken away the Lord out of the sepulchre, and we know not where they have laid Him.

Peter therefore went forth, and that other disciple; and came to the sepulcher.

So they both ran together to the sepulchre, and the other disciple did outran Peter and came first to the sepulchre.

John 20:1-4

I have personally read this chapter at least one hundred times. One day when I was going through a faith trial, it revealed to me a whole different light; the point that stuck out was that "They ran while it yet was still dark." To understand the title of this chapter, you would have to understand the personal issues that these biblical characters faced and how it interrelates to you as a person.

Israel had awaited their Messiah and King who would deliver them from the tyranny of the Roman government, and the disciples believed that this King was Jesus. All of their hopes and dreams of deliverance were wrapped up in Him, and now He is dead.

Have you ever had the experience where you have put all your emotions, dreams, visions into something, and you look at it and it appears dead? One mind is telling you, "Give up" the other mind is saying, "Run, run even though it's still dark." The thing is dead, but your faith won't accept its death. At this point, you are running while it's still dark.

Now, what's mysterious is, and if you accept the Bible as 100% truth, God painfully goes out of the way to tell you about a race between Peter and John, while describing the most amazing feat in the history of this world, The Resurrection. God says that John outran Peter. What is God trying to tell the reader of this passage? John represented "faith" and "relationship;" while Peter represented "unbelief," so "faith" reached the empty tomb first.

What is God trying to communicate to the reader right now, at this exact moment, hour and second, as you read this manuscript? Trust Him when you can't trace Him. God is saying:
Although you didn't get that position in politics that you prayed for, run while it's still dark!
Although you came home and the foreclosure sign is on the door, run while it's still dark.
Although you went to court and your appeal was denied, run while it's still dark! Although you prayed over your marriage and the divorce papers came in the mail, run while it's still dark!
Although your foster home is worse than the home you left because you were abused, run while it's still dark!

You have believed God for some things (you have called some things that be not as if they were,) and behind your back people are whispering about you saying, "You are crazy!" Run while yet it's still dark! He left you, she left you, heart crushed, can't sleep, can't eat, don't want to wake up...Run while it's dark!

Why all this running? It's simple. God said in the first chapter of the gospel of John:
"In the beginning, was the Word and the Word was with God and the Word was God."
"All things were made by Him, and without Him nothing was made."
"The Word was made flesh and lived amongst us."

So what is the writer John saying? Jesus is outside of creation and everything that was created, he made. So, if I trust an entity that is outside of creation, who created everything, then whatever I am going through He has the power to change since He created everything.

Now I know why John got to the grave before Peter.

Run while yet it's still dark!

35
INANIMATE OBJECTS CANNOT GIVE PEACE TO THE HUMAN SPIRIT

I open this chapter with a biblical account found in Mark 10:17-27 of a very young, rich Jewish ruler in pursuit of Jesus to ask him what more he could do to be happy and have eternal life.

How do we know he was Jewish? Jesus said to him in verse 19, *You know the commandments; the commandments were given to the Jews first."*

This man was so earnest in his appeal to Jesus that, after he admitted keeping the Ten Commandments he broke Jewish law by bowing to Jesus – calling him a good man and teacher. Jewish law required a man's life for relating to a mortal man in this way. This was a ground breaking decision. When this man did this publically in honor of Jesus, he was telling Christ that he believed he was God.

The Bible goes on to reveal that this man was challenged by Jesus to sell all his earthly goods and take up the Cross of Christ. It's important to point out that when he first approached Jesus, you get the sense he knew that inanimate objects (money, cars, houses, popularity) could not bring peace to the human spirit. Its equally sad to emphasize that although he acknowledged that Jesus was the Messiah he could not part with his money, fame, popularity and lifestyle, so he walked away sad.

Several years ago Deion Sanders, an athlete that I deeply admire, pulled to the side of the road and contemplated suicide. Why? This man seemed to have everything - money, fame, women, good looks, etc. Surprisingly, he was missing one important thing – PEACE! There are two different types of peace on this earth; world peace and God's gift of peace which surpasses all understanding. Deion Sanders was lacking the peace of God!

Exactly what is the peace of God? Well, to be brutally honest with you, the peace of God can be apprehended, but it's not easily comprehended. It's not unintelligible, but it has to be experiential; in other words, you must experience it to attempt to explain it. In essence it is unexplainable. God said in Philippians 4:7, *And the peace of God which surpasses all understanding shall guard your hearts and minds through Christ Jesus.*

In the New Testament account found in Mathew 14:22-23, Peter, a disciple of Christ was a Jew God manifested himself to through Old Testament scripture and physically through following Jesus Christ. Peter understood in the Book of Job 9:8 that Job attributes the phenomenon of walking on water to God alone. When Peter personally witnessed Jesus do so, he asked permission to come, thus acknowledging that Jesus was God. As you continue reading the story, as long as Peter had his eyes on Christ, he was just fine walking on the water; but when something happened, such as the wind got unruly, he took his eyes off Christ and began to sink. This peace was taken from him. The Bible says in Isaiah 26:3, *Those who keep their mind on the Lord, He will keep them in perfect peace."*

You see as long as you have God governing the affairs of your life, you can have peace. The majority of the peace comes from the fact that God exists outside of creation. Humans are inside creation, so anything that begins to exist, God has total sovereignty over (or totally controls). If Peter understood that concept and believed it, he would have never fell to his fear.

Deion Sanders almost ended it all because nothing material could give him peace. The average person reading this may chuckle and say, "Hey, give me twenty-five million dollars, good looks and fame. Trust me I will have peace. They may be right, because there are magnitudes of peace – our world's system for peace and the peace of God that comes from another dimension, not of this world.

Question: Well, can you explain the difference? Answer: I will do the best that I can.

First of all, we must agree on the fact that everything on this earth is cursed from humans to animals, etc. Everything created has an expiration date. Whatever pleasure that you get from something "material" is only temporary, because you were created eternal, to live forever. Whatever pleasure you get from something temporal will always leave a void in your heart that yearns for peace.

Have you ever watched the soap operas - *One Life to Live, All My Children, The Young and the Restless,* and so on? Have you ever wondered why affluent upper-class people stay depressed? Although on screen its acting, the actors are actually acting out real life drama. The soap operas mirror how real life is, operating under our world's system of peace that speaks like this:

- I must live in a gated guarded community, or I am a failure.
- I am not successful if I don't possess the American Dream (Wife, Husband, 2.2 kids, house with a white picket fence)
- One woman is not good enough for me.
- I need money, money, money!
- I must own a Mercedes or bust!
- If he is not making six figures, don't introduce me.
- Money, power, respect is the key of life.

That is the world's system and language. When the Great Depression hit at the turn of the century most successful people living under this system committed suicide. The world's viewpoint of what brings peace involves torment. Deion Sanders' torment led him to Christ.

Well, how can money, good looks and fame be tormenting? It's not that these things are bad. I would be a hypocrite if I said they were. What I was equating is they cannot bring you peace. For example, if you take an inner city child from the ghetto, and place them in an affluent suburban home and gave them every material desire of their heart, that child would be incomplete. How can I say that? That child would exchange gun violence and drugs for the quiet, serene law abiding atmosphere. That child would exchange full course meals and new clothes for poverty and malnutrition. The child would swap a complete home with two moral, attentive parents, for a drug addicted mother and a father who is in jail.

How in the world could I say the child is incomplete? Easily! Imagine putting that child to bed. It's a cold winter night. The child had an excellent day. Life is perfect for the child. The snow flakes are falling on the trees. Deer and rabbits are scurrying about and it's quiet. You check in on the child, and the child is lying on his / her back staring at the sky teary eyed. You kneel next to the child and ask them him/her what's wrong. The child, with eyes full of tears sits there speechless, but nods their head suggesting nothing is wrong. You recite a list of things you gave them, and suggest that if that's not enough, you will give them even more. You state, "Please tell me what's wrong!" Then the child screams from the bottom chambers of their heart, "I want my mommy, I want my daddy!" The couple then comes to the stark reality that inanimate objects cannot bring peace to the human soul.

The child had all the trappings of life. A good home, safe environment, good foster parents, etc. One thing was missing, their biological parents; their D.N.A., their creator.

No matter whether you are:
- Beyonce Knowles
- A Go-Go dancer at a bar
- A construction worker, living from paycheck to paycheck
- A drug addict, or clinical supervisor of the drug treatment program

You will never have peace until you come into an intimate relationship with the one who formed you, shaped you, breathed life into you and called you into existence. Because inanimate objects by their very nature are fallible, flawed, temporal and can never bring you peace. You are an eternal being. So, everything you are looking for in temporal objects can be found in an ETERNAL GOD...PEACE!

36
WHAT ABOUT ME

Recently after finalizing the manuscript of this book, my marketing agent texted me after reading it and estimating that in the first two years five million copies would be sold. He went further, stating how revelatory the book was and how it hit every area of human need. At the same time, a good friend of mine named Kevin walked in the school where I worked to tell me that he read my first book and how he couldn't wait for the next book to come out. Bubbling with joy, I showed him the text from my marketing agent. He looked and said "Wow Monty, you are really doing it, aren't you?" I replied, 'Yup, thank God.' As I began to discuss the chapters and the content of the book with him, Kevin seemed naturally excited for me; but as he left, it seemed as if he left with a void. The book gave a hope for every area in life, but it didn't give a hope for death. *What about me.*

You see Kevin had had a "Job" experience. Kevin lost three sons, a nephew, mother, and father in a span of six years. Each incident happened year by year. So each time he attempted to recover from one death, here came another one. I asked Kevin, 'How could you endure such pain, agony, despair, grief and hopelessness and walk around every day with a smile on your face.' Then he took me into deep waters. Kevin began to ask me some very deep penetrating questions:

"Hey Monty, would you say the disciples were cowards before Christ's resurrection?"

I responded, 'Uh, yes and no.'

He responded, "It is not a yes or no question. Scripture says in Matthew 26:56 that *"all the disciples forsook Jesus and ran.* Were they cowards or not?"

I responded, 'Since you put it that way the answer is yes.'

"Now post resurrection would you say they were cowards or lions?"

I responded, "Lions. All were martyred except John, so the scripture could be fulfilled.'

Kevin responded, "Why the transformation. What changed in the disciples that they went from cowards to lions each and every one of them?"

I responded 'Kevin, I know where you are going with this but the disciples were not the only people who died for their faith. How about Islamic extremists?'

He replied, "It is conceivable for a person to die for what he believed was true, but it is inconceivable for a person to die for what he knew was a lie. When Christ rose from the dead he gave assurance that all who believed in Him would rise in like manner and because my family believed in Him I will see them again. That's why I smile everyday, all day."

I dropped my head and smiled. Wow, what a revelation, what a hope.

As I began to exhort him for the revelation, he said something that resonated in my spirit, "Hey Monty, I know what you are thinking? How could my sons and nephew go to heaven when they were drug dealers and of another faith?"

I responded, 'Kevin, I am not going to fake you out, you read my mind verbatim.'

Kevin responded "Hey Monty, you have your Bible?"

I said, 'Yes, I never leave home without it.'

He said, "Go to Luke 23:39-43."

After I read it he began to give me the revelation.

"Hey Monty, how many criminals were on the cross?"

'Two'

"How many went to heaven?"

'One'

"Why did he go to heaven?"

'Because he acknowledged Jesus as Jehovah and asked Jesus to save him.'

"Did the criminal have good works?"

'Not according to Luke 23:41. He said he deserved death.'

"What were Jesus' last words to this man?"

'Assuredly this day you will be with me in paradise.'

I replied, 'Kevin I don't want to grieve your spirit, but how do you know they called on Jesus?'

He replied, "With each death there was a witness. Miraculously each witness said that my sons and nephews called on the name of Jesus before they took their last breath. Scripture says in Romans 10:13, *Whoever calls on the name of the Lord will be saved.* (Drug dealers, murderers, child molesters, rapist, prostitutes, gangsters, whoremongers, liars and cheaters, Muslims, Buddhist, Hindus and Sikhs…)

Kevin then continued, "Monty, do you know what the great joy is in heaven? It is physical." Kevin, then in an ecstatic trance said, "Hey Monty, remember when Jesus appeared to the disciples after His resurrection?" "What did he say?" "Behold my hands and my feet, that it is I." "Handle me and see for a spirit does not have flesh and bones as you see I have."

"Do you get it? Jesus was telling the disciples if you and the world have faith in ME, you will appear to your love ones in like manner, physical. No deformities, same race, same language, whatever made you cry about yourself will be made perfect; people born with no arms and legs will have arms and legs, people born blind will have sight, people born orphaned will have parents, people born in 3rd world countries who suffered will laugh."

"No Monty, far from what Hollywood and some of these churches depict. You will be flying around with white wings floating in the air; no, no, no. Heaven is going to be a blast - a physical blast."

Then Kevin said, "Hey Monty, have you ever heard that CD by Eric Clapton, *Tears in Heaven?*

I said, 'Yes, vaguely.'

Then Kevin began to hum a few bars. Kevin wasn't the greatest singer but never the less I received the revelation. Eric Clapton lost his son in a tragic accident. Because children automatically inherit heaven, Eric began to sing about Heaven and one of the questions he asked in the song was "Would you know my name if I saw you in heaven, would it be the same if I saw you in heaven?" The answer is YES! Eric will see his son if he placed faith in the God of the Bible. Will it be the same? Absolutely not; when Eric see his son not only will his tears be turned into joy, but his son will never experience death again, and neither will Eric Clapton.

What a sensible blessed hope!! Everything lost will be restored.

The Miles Theory

Recently, I overheard a conversation between my sister and my brother-in-law Clarence Miles. We call him Miles. Miles is a dreamer, and I don't mean this in a condescending way, but he just aspires to a lofty lifestyle which I believe is perfectly fine as long as God is primary in your life. Miles made this statement "Hey, I better hurry up and get my yacht because according to the movie *2012* the end will be here soon."

It's a pity that Miles' thinking is so distorted, but it is a travesty that 90% of the world population of 7 billion think heaven is boring. Let's examine Miles theory in light of scripture:

First, the Bible says in I Corinthians 2:9 that "Eyes haven't seen, ears haven't heard and it hasn't entered the imagination of man what God has in store for those who love Him." So what is God saying? Hey Miles, you see that 100 million dollars yacht that you went bananas over, take that yacht multiply it times 121,666 and after you have done that math it still doesn't compare to what I have planned for you. Jesus couldn't have said it more clearly in John 14:2, *In my Father's house are many mansions, if it were not so, I would have told you. I go to prepare a place for you.*

Let me ask you a few questions:

Who was the Bible written to?
- The Jews

Who was the Bible written for?
- The world

So the YOU in John 14:2 is every human with a soul that believes. The Bible says in Psalms 37:4, *Delight yourself in the Lord, and He will give you the very desires of your heart.* Well, since God is our Creator and He knows what our inward part desires, then Jesus being God, when He said *I go to prepare a place for YOU* means that every moral desire of your heart will be fulfilled!

For example, let's say you love to swim. Would it be a stretch for God to have the Atlantic Ocean as your Jacuzzi? Let's say you like to ski, would it be possible for God to give you the Swiss Alps in your backyard?

Now you may say to yourself "I, the author, may need a drug test or I have a fertile imagination, but actually it's neither. I'm taking God out of the box and stretching my imagination as far as it will go because He said "Eyes have not seen, nor ears heard…" but we have a clue, and the clue is eyes have not seen, ears have not heard compared to what? The answer is, compared to what you have seen and heard on this earth. Even when I attempt to stretch my imagination it pales in comparison to what God has for those who love Him. Additionally, I want you to think about this, how many days did it take God to create the world? The Answer: six days. Jesus said in John 14:1-3 that He is going to prepare a place for us or a new world.

Question:

Is this world absolutely opulent?
- Yes

If this opulent world took six days to make, exactly what type of world is Jesus preparing and he has been preparing it for the last 2000 years?
- Well, one would have to multiply 2000 years by 365 days and that comes out to 730,000 days divided by six days which equals 121,666 days which equal "Eyes have not seen ears have not heard and it haven't entered the heart of man the things that God has prepared for those who love Him."

So if Miles was thinking theologically, he would be saying Jesus hurry up! Don't delay!

Last two points about heaven's physicality:

Question:

What was Lucifer's position in heaven?
- He was the chief angel.

What was Lucifer adorned with?
- Diamonds, Rubies, Beryl and all types of precious stones.

When Lucifer rebelled where did God cast him down to?
- God cast him into the Garden of Eden.

Geographically according to the Bible, where is the Garden of Eden today?
- On the continent of Africa.

What continent has the greatest supply of precious stones on earth?
- Africa.

If Lucifer fell from heaven and landed in Africa is it a total stretch to surmise that all the trillions of diamonds discovered in Africa fell off of Lucifer? Now Lucifer is not made in the image of God, nor has a covenant with God. If God did that for Lucifer, what does he have in store for his personal children?

Look at the front cover of this book. Look at the woman that's hugging the man, and look at the man beside her. What do you see? Do you see what I see? I see two people having an out of body experience. I see a couple who put their son or daughter to bed last night, read them a story-book, and then talked about Christmas and Santa Claus. I see a couple who woke their children up for school, ate breakfast with them and promised to pick them up after school. Never in a million years did they think that they would be planning their children's funeral.

As I focus on the man looking up towards the heavens, I can only attempt to read his mind. The first thing he's saying is, "Let this be a nightmare God!" The second is, "Why me?" "How could you allow this to happen…My baby, my baby, I will never again see my baby!"

You know all religions have a hope attached to it, and I respect each religion's belief system; but there comes a time where the rubber meets the road.

Buddhism says when you die, you are reincarnated, so if that be true you may come back as the killer, or that wouldn't resolve the look and horror on the family's face because they didn't get back what they lost.

In Jehovah Witness theology, only 144,000 will make it to heaven. Now we are faced with a statistical dilemma, because there is no guarantee if the twenty children from Sandy Hook made it to heaven that their parents would make it to heaven also.

Mormonism doesn't ring the bell, because it tells the family that they will appear before the heavenly father (God) dressed in fig leaves and aprons holding good works in their hands. Virtually everyone qualifies for heaven un-repentant; whoremongers, murderers and the vilest people on earth make it to the Terrestrial heaven. If that is the hope then you are bound to run into gunman Adam Lanza again, un-repentant.

I believe what's most sensible and reasonable is not only to see their son or daughter again, but to see them as the same race, nationality, color, speaking the same language, never to experience death or pain again.

While writing this book and attempting to process this horrific tragedy (please remember I am referring to the couple depicted on this book's cover), God led me to two scriptures, Revelations 7:9 and Revelations 21:4.

In Revelations 7:9, the Bible says, *After these things I looked, and behold, a great multitude which no man could number from every nation, tribe, people and tongue.*

This passage of scripture speaks about salvation at the end of time and it basically says to the family in Sandy Hook, Connecticut and anyone else whoever suffers tragedy that you will see your loved ones again physically; same race, same language and same nationality.

Just imagine at the end of this age, which may be very, very soon, that parents of the children of Sandy Hook physically going to the malls, or eating dinner or going on a vacation with the children that they lost in that tragedy.

If the parents were saying to God, "Why did you let this happen to us? Why me?" What in the heavens will they say to God when He returns back the physical bodies of their loved ones never to experience crying, death or pain again? Moreover, not just the children of Sandy Hook, but the children in Syria, India, Africa, dialysis patients, AIDS patients, cancer patients, or loved ones lost to senseless gang or gun violence to come back to this earth never to experience pain or death again.

This is the only answer that will heal the couple on the front of this book and any other human no matter what religion; whether you are Buddhist, Muslim, Jews, Cabbalist, Zoastrist, Jehovah's Witness, Mormon, or atheist. God then ties Revelations 21:4 where it says, *And God will wipe away every tear from their eyes; there shall be no more death, nor sorrow, nor crying. There shall be no more pain, for the former thing has passed away.*

If you revert back to the image of the man and woman and the man looking up at the heavens the only reasonable hope in the world is the hope that God offers in Revelations 7:9 and 21:4.

God sums it up best by saying my Son died and was resurrected for this purpose. The same manner my Son resurrected physically and continues to live eternally, so is the hope for the victims of Sandy Hook and any other human who places faith in the Son of God.

The horror and tragedy of that day will never haunt you again because what you thought was lost is now found.

37
WHERE DO WE GO FROM HERE

The most important questions a human can ask is not what college will I go to? Who will I marry? What am I going to name my children? Where will I work? Where will I live? How many pounds am I going to lose?

The most important question is where am I going when I die?

This is the question that breaks the illusion of religions, cults and atheistic belief. This is where the rubber meets the road, and there is no middle ground for conjecture. Religion dissipates and the acidic questions, Am I saved or lost? Will I live or Die, get answered.

When a man dies, whether by gunshot wound, atomic explosion, cancer or eaten by a Great White Shark, his soul and his spirit separate and travel to two separate places. The body is placed in a grave and the spirit goes directly to God, no matter if you are Adolf Hitler or Martin Luther King. The soul goes to one of two destinations; if it is "saved" it goes directly to Paradise. If it is "unsaved," it goes directly to Hades (not to be confused with the Abyss or the Lake of Fire) just an intermediate place to await judgment.

Now as the spirit is eternal, so is the soul. The spirit has what's called a "soulish" body. This type of body can see, feel, thirst, talk and remember as proven in the biblical story of Lazarus in Luke 16:19-31. This is not a parable but a true depiction of what happens to the soul and spirit when a human dies. Both their physical bodies were left on the earth. What happened to them in their "spirit" state? They were both conscious. The rich man recognized Lazarus, and that it would have been impossible to do absent a physical body. This is proof that the soulish body is not simply a ghost-like body but in its outward form and appearance, it conforms to the earthly body of its owner. This proves that there is no break in the soul as it passes from earth life to spirit life – it continues to live.

To support this theory, I want to discuss the Germ Theory with you. If you ever read the contents on a bottle of disinfectant or common household cleaner it almost always says Kills 99% of household germs – whether it be Lysol, Mr. Clean, PineSol or Clorox. This supports the theory in modern science that in every human body there is a LIVING GERM that is indestructible; and though the body turns to dust that "living germ" will continue to exist in the grave or wherever a dead body is deposited. Like a seed in the ground it will spring into eternal life without end when the time of the resurrection of the body shall come. The Bible, in Mark 9:44, refers to this germ as the "eternal worm that never dies."

While closing out this book I experienced three major deaths of people very close to me: two of my closest friends and my mother, Mary McLaurin. I often pondered how I would handle the death of a close friend, but never did I ever consider how I would handle my mother dying; I would break down and cry, not only is it natural, it's biblical. For some strange reason I could not find the tears.

On Tuesday, October 15, 2013 I was hosting my radio ministry,

Reasons 4 Hope. A faithful caller, Sister Shirley called in to testify about her mother's death. At the conclusion of the show as I signed off, the phone rang. I picked up the phone and my sister Marilyn said, "Mommy died!" I looked at my co-host Clarence Miles, and said "Mommy died, let's go get some shrimp."

Telephoned calls and texts poured in. My daughter Lauren and son Lamont called and gave their condolences, and so did friends, family, etc. I anticipated a breakdown. For some unforeseen reason I could not find the tears. I said to myself maybe when I get with my family it will hit me. When I did so, it still had not hit me.

The following Tuesday was the day of mom's home going service at St. John's A.M.E Church. I had to give remarks. I thought then would be the time that I would breakdown. On that day, my family and I walked into and later out of the funeral without tears. One might say, "Oh, so what, so your family faked their emotions – who can't do that?" Actually that's the farthest from the truth; my family is tight knit and we all had a very close relationship with my mother. The thing is, we all understood death.

Jesus said these words in the Book of St. John 11:25-26, I am the resurrection and the life; he that believeth in me, though he were dead, yet shall he live! And whosoever liveth and believeth in ME shall never die.

So at its taproot, the answers to the questions "Where do I go when I die?" and "Will I live forever where I am going is YES, but the choice is yours. The Bible is crystal clear in the Book of Acts 4:12:

Neither is their salvation in any other, for there is no other name under heaven given among men, whereby we must be saved.

38
YOU CAN'T STOP ME, YOU CAN ONLY HOPE TO CONTAIN ME

When I think of the title of this chapter, I think of two basketball players: Michael Jordan and Kobe Bryant. Then I think of the life of a person who is seriously pursuing a relationship with God due to some type of hardship or tribulation.

If you ever watch an opposing team strategize for Michael or Kobe you will always hear the coaches say, "Hey look, Michael or Kobe is going to get their 30 points. Just make sure you don't let him get out of control and to shut the rest of the team down." That is exactly the way a life of a believer is designed. You cannot stop them. You can only hope to contain them.

At the start of the Book of Job, Job was living life his way; then all of a sudden calamity and catastrophe arose in his life to the degree where Job's own wife said, "Why don't you curse God and die?" But because Job held on to his integrity and faith at the end of the story God gave him double for his trouble; more money, prestige, children, wisdom, peace and more joy. You see Satan tried to stop Job when he incited Job's wife to say curse God and die, but he could only contain him.

Containment is a period you go through, and I thank God for them because without tribulation we could never know the fullness of joy. Remember it's not the setback, it's the get back. Like a true believer, you can't stop them; you can only hope to contain them.

Romans Chapter 8 is one of the most encouraging books in the entire Bible. It starts off with no condemnation, in the middle it says God is fighting for you and the end says no separation. How can you lose this battle? You were set up to be blessed. Heaven and earth will pass away if God doesn't answer your prayer. The victory is guaranteed. The fix is in. God said He placed His word above His name.

God specializes in taking the sick, weak and the "nobodies" of this world and getting His glory through them. You are well on you road to recovery. God is going to do a new thing in you! If He told you, your ears would tingle! God said in Jeremiah 33:3 I will show you great and mighty things that you do not know.

Its break through time and this isn't itching ears, "feels good talk." If it is your season, you have a reason to get excited. Even if it's not your season, get excited like Christmas is coming. I hope your enemies are prepared for their new occupation, yes they will be your personal footstools. Yes, it definitely gets great later but you must get through the worst first!

You can't stop me. You can only hope to contain me!

Now unto him that is able to do exceeding abundantly above all that we ask or think, according to the power that worketh in us. (Ephesians 3:20)

39
CAN I TRUST THE BIBLE

The Bible is the most indicted book in the history of mankind. Some say the Bible is tampered with. Some say parts are true and parts are false. Some say Jewish people wrote it to control people, and a whole host of other preposterous allegations that have proven to be demonstratively false. **It is critical that we learn to question that the indictment is valid.** The attitude to approach the Bible with should be the same attitude that we deal with our citizens in the American Court system; It is critical that we learn to question the indictment rather than assume the indictment is valid.

The Bible doesn't just say, "Hey, I am truth believe me!" It proves that it is true and then says believe me. Well how does the Bible prove itself to be divine and not human in nature? The Bible proves itself in many ways. Here are four significant ways:

1. Predictive Prophecy
2. Science of Statistical Data
3. Manuscript Evidence
4. Logical Deduction

Let's first deal with the origin of the Bible. The Bible through logical deduction could have been written by only one of five sources.

1. Good Men & Angels
2. Bad Men & Demons
3. God

Let's examine each of these categories:

Good Men & Angels:
How could a man reputed as good dedicate his entire life to writing an entire book of lies that says "Thus says the Lord" and still be considered good. That disqualifies good men and Angels.

Bad Men & Demons

Name three evil men.
   1) Hitler
   2) Stalin
   3) Iddi Amin Da-Da

Question: What makes them evil?

Answer: Their works. How could evil men devote their entire life to a book that encourages you to love your neighbor, fear God, and do good? Evil men would be denying themselves. They would cease to be evil. How do you know Hitler was the author of *Mein Kampf*? The contents of the book were consistent with his personality.

Now, since the categories evil men & demons, good men & Angels have been deleted, we are left with one person. GOD!

The Bible says in II Peter 1:20, 21, *Knowing this first, that no prophecy of scripture is of any private interpretation.*

For the prophecy came not by the will of men but holy men of God spake as they were moved by the Holy Spirit.

Predictive Prophecy

Several times in scripture, the Bible stresses the use of prophecy to determine if something is of God.

Deuteronomy 18:22: *When a prophet speaketh in the name of the LORD, if the thing follow not, nor come to pass, that is the thing which the LORD hath not spoken, but the prophet hath spoken it presumptuously: thou shalt not be afraid of him.*

Have you ever had the experience of sending a Western Union to another person or transferring money from bank to bank? When making these transactions, you will always be issued a secret code to give to the recipient of the transaction. Why a secret code? The reason that it is a secret is because it verifies that you received the information from the direct source. That's how the Bible uses predictive prophecy. The Bible speaks of things 5,000 years ago, and yet you can read them in the Daily News tomorrow. Certainly, men cannot guess that well, so we know that when the prophets speak and things come to pass, it's from God and God alone.

For example, many of these prophecies would have been impossible for Jesus to deliberately conspire to fulfill such as:

1. His descent from Abraham, Isaac and Jacob (Genesis 12:3, 17:19, Matthew 1:1-2, Acts 3:25)
2. His birth in Bethlehem (Micah 5:2, Matthew 2:1-6)
3. His crucifixion with criminals (Isaiah 53:12, Matthew 27:38, Luke 22:37)
4. The piercing of His hands and feet on the cross (Psalm 22:16, John 20:25)
5. The soldiers gambling for His clothes (Psalm 22:18, Matthew 27:35)
6. The piercing of His side (Zechariah 12:10, John 19:34)
7. The fact that His bones were not broken at His death (Psalm 34:20, John 19:33-37)
8. His burial among the rich (Isaiah 53:9, Matthew 27:57-60)

In sharp contrast, predictive prophecy demonstrates the divine origin of the Bible where all other holy books are conspicuous by its absence.

Well, how about Nostradamus. He was a seer and a prophet wasn't he? Didn't he predict the rise of Hitler and Germany in the 1500's? The answer is a resounding NO! The problem with Nostradamus and so many other psychic predictions is that they are always inaccurate ambiguous and confusing.

Let's look at Nostradamus' quatrain or prediction:

Followers of sects, great trouble are in store for the messenger. A beast upon the theater prepares the scenically play. The inventor of that wicked feat will be famous. By sects the world will be confused and divided. Beast mad with hunger will swim across rivers. Most of the army will be against the Lower Danube (Hitler sera) the great one will be dragged in an iron cage when the child brother (de Germain) will observe nothing.

- Now obviously, this is not a reference to Adolf Hitler. The word isn't Hitler but Hister, and it is clearly not a person but a place. The Latin phrase de Germain should be interpreted as a brother or near relative not Germany.

- He doesn't recite dates, time frames, and what does he mean by beast and iron cages? The prediction is so confusing until it's meaningless.

There's nothing like the prophetic specificity of the Bible. Genesis 16:7, 12 is one of my favorite, talking about the Arab nation. God first tells the mother of the Arabs that they will be a great nation but will not be the multitude. Right on point! Today's census last I checked was 6.7 billion people; 1.2 billion are Muslims, 2.9 billion are Christians. The rest are different sects. God made Ishmael great but not the multitude.

'He shall be a wild man." What does God mean by wild? They would be extremists. If you've ever studied Arab history, you'll know if they love you, they will love you extremely, but if they hate you they will hate you extremely.

Let's look at the descents of the gentlemen below.

1. Saddam Hussein
2. Yasaar Arafat
3. Ayatollah Khomeini
4. Hijackers of 911
5. Osama Bin Laden

Question: What descent are these men?

Answer: Arab.

Question: What personality traits do they have in common?

Answer: They all are extremely serious men that you wouldn't want to cross the wrong way.

God makes other astounding predictions. God named Ishmael in Chapter 16 before he was born and described his character while in the womb. In Genesis 17:20 God tells Abraham before Ishmael is born, how many sons he will have (Genesis 25:12 (which later translated into nations). God also told Abraham that Ishmael would be rich or fruitful. *Now this prophecy was uttered approximately 4,000 years ago!* When did the Arabs become financially prosperous? It was 4,000 years later in the 20th Century through commercial oil. Wow! I am in awe of predictive prophecy - the Bible said it 4,000 years ago and it comes to pass today. The only thing more awe inspiring in this text is the Writer.

Who was the writer of Genesis?

It was Prophet Moses. When was Moses born? About 1650 B.C. Well, how could Moses know about Abraham, Ishmael and the creation account if he wasn't even born at the time? There is only one answer. God spoke to him. There are no Jean Dixons, Nostradamus, crystal balls, horoscopes or the like that can predict the future like the Bible.

Need more proof?

When you study the science of statistical data you go into the realm of possibility and improbabilities based on statistical facts.

When you look at biblical prophecy the writers could not have achieved such unbelievable accuracy unless God revealed to them what to write. The most ardent skeptic may need more proof.

1. First, the odds against fallible men predicting the future on their own without God stagger the imagination.

2. Picture the entire state of Texas covered in silver dollars two feet deep. One of those silver dollars is specially marked. Blindfold someone and ask him/her to walk across the state for a few weeks and then randomly select that one silver dollar. What are the chances of success? Only 1 in 10/28.

3. Now picture the vast continent of Africa and Asia covered in silver two feet deep. Ask someone to walk a few years and then randomly select one special marked coin. That's 1 in 10/39

The point is in a hundred billion years there is no chance that the statistical accuracy of biblical prophecy ever would have been fulfilled unless God chose to step into human history and communicate His word to men.

Manuscript Evidence

Because of my vocation as a theologian, I have encountered many reasoning sessions or debates with men from other religions. One of the most prevalent discussions is the assertion that the Bible has been tampered with. Whether Muslim, Hindu, Buddhist Krishna, Moonies or Cultic Christians sects they almost always present the empirically fallacious saying, *we believe in the Bible, but only the parts that haven't been tampered with.* Well my response is very simple but woefully devastating: *Can you show me where the Bible is tampered with in the Old and New Testament, chapter and verse?* Almost always there is a moment of silence followed by this response, *Well, I don't know where, but I know it is tampered with.*

Wow! Can you imagine someone bringing an indictment of that magnitude against you with absolutely no proof and you would have to bear the consequence of the accusation? Wouldn't you agree that if you or your family members were incarcerated for thirty years for a person's notion that you would suffer a terrible injustice? If your answer is "yes" then what about God?

Years ago, I was working for a well known lawyer in Philadelphia as an investigator on a case that involved counterfeit money. Later as the government presented their case, they first explained the indictment to the jury. They then compared the real money to the fake money and convicted the defendant.

If the Bible was tampered with, and since it has been the number one best selling book in the world, why hasn't someone stepped forward with the evidence of tampering and who tampered with it? **There's only one reason. The Bible is 100% true.**

One of the greatest witnesses of the Bible being true is manuscript evidence, the greatest proof being the Dead Sea Scrolls. It's story begins like this:

In the spring of 1947, an Arab lad Mohammed-Ad-Dhib was herding goats in the area of the Dead Sea in Israel, when one of the goats ran into a cave. Mohammed subsequently threw a stone in the cave to scare the goat into coming out. The stone broke a jar, frightening the lad away. The lad returned with a companion, entered the cave and found several scrolls wrapped in pottery jars.

The lad brought the scrolls back to Bethlehem to sell. After several disappointing attempts, he sold some to Professor E.L. Sunekik of the Hebrew University and the balance to Metropolitan Samuel of St. Marks Syrian Orthodox Monastery. Inside the scrolls contained the Book of Isaiah, Habakkuk, Genesis, Deuteronomy, Psalms, Samuel, Numbers, Leviticus, Jeremiah and Ruth.

In each scroll, not one part of the text was changed. The Book of

Isaiah you read today is the same Isaiah that was placed there nearly 2,700 years ago, written 2,700 years ago. Since the phenomenon cannot be reasoned or explained away, we can safely, reasonably and intelligently conclude that because of these factors and many more infallible proofs that the Bible is the Word of God, the proof is inescapable.

The entirety of Your word is truth. (Psalm 119:160)

Therefore say, Thus saith the Lord GOD; Although I have cast them far off among the heathen, and although I have scattered them among the countries, yet will I be to them as a little sanctuary in the countries where they shall come. (16).

Therefore say, Thus saith the Lord GOD; I will even gather you from the people, and assemble you out of the countries where ye have been scattered, and I will give you the land of Israel. (17). (Ezekiel 11:16-17)

Now if that doesn't leave you spellbound, these next exhibits of prophecy will tear you completely out the frame.

About 2,700 ago the Prophet Ezekiel spoke about a diaspora (or dispersion) that would happen to God's chosen people, the Jews. If you just took a cursory examination of the scriptures, you will observe that God predicted three exact things 2,700 years ago.

1. I am going to cast you off into the countries
2. I am going to gather you back.
3. I am going to give you the land.

In 70 A.D., Titus the emperor of Rome pillaged Israel. The Jews left Israel dispersed through the four corners of the earth, (specifically May 14, 1948) and 1900 years later by a divine miracle, the word of God spoken 2,600 years ago, came to pass. How could this be if Almighty God didn't see the future and write the future in His Book? The only thing more awe inspiring than the Bible is the writer, who is God Almighty!

40
DID YOU HEAR ABOUT LAMONT

Fifty years ago, my late mother prayed to God, and this was her prayer; "Lord, if you give me a male child, I will dedicate his life to you." After five tries, the prayer was answered and an eight pound, eight ounce baby boy, me - Lamont McLaurin, manifested!

As far back as I can remember, in my own quirky way I was searching for God. One day while taking a bath, I was bored and began speaking to God. I said 'God am I going to be a good little boy and never break the law or sell drugs or do bad things like that?' Immediately after I said this, it began to pour down, raining with thundering. One of my sisters, now my pastor overheard me and began to chuckle endearingly, as if to say "Aww."

As time moved on, God began to manifest himself to me. One day, while playing in Fairmount Park with some neighborhood kids, I fell off a cliff. As I looked up, I saw my four sisters praying, frantically pleading for God to save me. The reason they were screaming was because I was about 75 pounds, holding onto a very thin branch and if I didn't get rescued, I would have had a 200 foot drop into the Schuylkill River. Let's say I had a 99% chance of dying! Moments later, a bold young lady named, Faye reached down with one hand and lifted me up to safety. A crowd jumped for joy and relief! The sky became eerily dark, a brisk wind came through, and we watched the wind blow the branch I held onto into the atmosphere. In amazement, the crowd in a sort of trance watched this branch until it disappeared into the Heavens. The branch never came to the ground! On the way back home, one of the onlookers asked, "How could a skinny little branch, hold a 75 pound kid and then the wind come by and sweep the branch away? That was an act of God!"

Seven years later, I was down in North Carolina with my father, Robert McLaurin. My father was the type of man that thought young males from big cities were passive or sissies. He used to always condemn or compare me to my cousins who were from the South. One day while fishing with my cousins Pierre, Laval and my dad at Carolina Beach, my cousins were reeling in fish one after the other. I began to feel despondent. My dad was cheering them on, while I was standing at the mouth of the ocean, with my fishing rod in the water looking like the loneliest kid in the world. Because of my embarrassment and stress, I began to pray. I didn't know God's name, nor did I know who God was at the time. But I said this to Him, 'Please God, I am so embarrassed. If I don't catch a fish, I am going to look like a wuss, and they are going to tease me!' A voice came from Heaven, I lie to you not, and said, "Walk fifty feet east and cast your rod." As I did what the voice said, I felt a tug on my rod. I began to holler, 'I got one, I got one, I got one!' As I began to reel the hook in, there were three butter fish on the hook with a mysterious branch tangled into the line that looked exactly like the branch that was holding me up on the cliff!

On the way home, the cliff incident and the fishing incident played heavily on my mind. The entire trip home I was quiet, thinking about the two incidents and God. When we finally got home, my aunt Geraldine began to clean the fish and cook them. After dinner she said, "Monty, I tell you the truth, I have never tasted fish like that. You must have gotten them straight from Heaven!"

A few years passed by. At my afterschool job as a busboy for IHOP in Lower Merion, PA, I met a man named Jeremiah Shabazz. He said, "Hey kid, how would you like to make some money?" I responded glassy eyed, 'Doing what?' He said, "Becoming the heavyweight champion of the world." He then gave me his business card and a full fledged relationship started. Minister Jeremiah was Muhammad Ali's administrative assistant. He took me from Spain to Maine. "Jeremiah was larger than life. I was with him one time in the early 1980's when he traveled to New York to settle a matter concerning Reverend Al Sharpton's life. My memory escapes me, but Al Sharpton was in trouble with the Italian Mafia. Jeremiah went to the boss of the Jewish Mafia, the Jewish Mafia met with the Italian Mafia and the matter was squashed, just by his word. I was there. I was awestruck by that undertaking. We built a father / son relationship, and I began seeking his God.

Jeremiah was a Muslim minister from the Nation of Islam, and like all ministers from the Nation he was sharp, charismatic, witty and a masterful orator. When a man is first born he does not know who God is, but by nature must worship something; so I began my quirky search. One day while Minister Shabazz was preaching, he taught that the white man was the devil. Since I had never been around whites before, I only knew of the volatile relationship with blacks and whites through history, movies, etc. I said to myself, 'Maybe he has a point.' But as time passed, I became skeptical of his God. One day, he told me that his wife (God bless her soul) was half Jewish. So I said within myself, if the white man is the devil, then Jeremiah's wife is 50% devil and his beautiful children were 25% devil too. I began to ponder, but yet still followed.

A year later, I found myself at Madison Square Garden, listening to one of Jeremiah's contemporaries, Minister Louis Farrakhan, a beast of an orator. He spoke of the suffering and oppression of black people. He reiterated approximately forty times that the white man was the "devil." At the very climax of the speech I was ready to give Louis Farrakhan a well deserved round of applause - until he made this statement, "But if he (the white man) gives us money and land, then he is our brother." The crowd jumped up applauding un-objectively, but I sunk in my chair. On the long ride home, I asked myself 100 times how could money and land change the nature of a devil?

A few months passed while I pondered the Madison Square Garden incident. I was invited to Washington, D.C. to meet with boxing legend Muhammad Ali, his wife, the richest man in the world at that time - Adnan Kashoggi, and a host of other famous people; this was organized by Jeremiah Shabazz. Needless to say, I was overtaken and awestruck by Mr. Kashoggis' entourage, the storybook beauty of wealthy Arab women and the host of stars and dignitaries.

While the big boys were out fraternizing, I was appointed to keep Ali's wife company. Lonnie was a woman with a quiet spirit and freckles; she reminded me of a big sister. At some point, boredom set in and I was asked to locate Muhammad Ali and the brothers that accompanied us. While searching the Summit Hotel, I came across the room that the brothers were in, and I observed at least four high ranking Muslim ministers having sex with white women, aka "white devils." **If Madison Square Garden was a blow, this was a bullet to the head!**

A few years later, I broke into the security industry by working at a club called *After Midnight*. Because of my leadership qualities, I quickly rose up the ranks and became the owner's personal body guard as well as head of security. This wasn't your average security team, it was mostly killers from every section of Philly with names like "Dave Henry," "Big Ock," "One-Arm-Marky," "Rock Money," "Scarface," "Sylvester," "Brisk," "Khalil," "Robert Bam Bam Hines," "Black Jesus," "D-Don," "Big T," "House-Wayne," "White Boy Kenny," "Big Phil," "Crazy Mark," "Bob Perry," of which I was boss.

The owner was a 6'5," 220 pound German American named Jim Helman. Jim influenced my life tremendously, because he was intelligent in the truest sense. Unlike some Caucasians who articulate the English language well and people say "Wow, he is intelligent" – he was diabolically intelligent. One day, a high ranking member of the Philly Mob approached Jim for the purpose of extortion; when he left, he not only left empty handed, but Jim turned around and extorted him. I learned every trick from Jim and Jeremiah and used them when the opportunity arose.

Two years passed. I was 19 years old and it was time for me to start searching for a career. I filled out an application for the Transit Police Department and got hired. That was the high point in my life before it turned dramatically wrong. While in the Transit Police Department, I made arrests that no other police officers in the department ever made even until this day but never was given any recognition or commendation. I was actually suspended one time for retrieving an officer's gun that was stolen from him and almost lost my life in an off-duty gun battle. As time passed by I started to lose my zeal for law enforcement. Guys from my academy class began to get better jobs outside of the department, but I just existed. One year passed by and a gentleman by the name of Roger Williams left Transit to go to the Philadelphia Police Department. His exodus had a draconian affect on me because Roger was my mentor. I looked up to him. He was always well groomed, well mannered with morals and ethics, the total package.

One night while working the night shift Sergeant John Arnold, who used to be my partner ask to sign my log. He then began to speak condescendingly to me and I responded very violently by threatening to kill him. I was fired for my actions and was rehired thirty days later; but when I came back, I came back "different." The devil had entered me. During my time out, my bills fell behind. I became very bitter, I began thinking of what I could have become if my talents were recognized in the department and how I was unjustly terminated. That's when after roll call I walked into the bathroom at 18th Street and John F. Kennedy Boulevard, and looked into the mirror and said these infamous words to myself, 'If you can't **beat** them, join them.' That is when my 11 year reign of terror started.

I began by robbing gang members called "wolf packs" after they would prey on subway riders; after all, who were they going to tell? I graduated to robbing drug dealers, mainly Hispanics who caught the subways at conspicuous stops wearing Temple and LaSalle hodies. I would lure them into conversations about sports, and then when the trains rolled up, I would take them into the bathroom, do a search, find the drugs and fake like I was calling the D.E.A. Once they start panicking, I separated the money from the drugs, picked up the money and asked them if they had all of their belongings. If they said yes, I would release them. If they said no, they were arrested. I never received a "No."

As time moved on, I began to be an expert at practicing lawlessness. I began to recruit thugs to handle my crimes - beatings, shootings, extortions, etc. I controlled my white collar business in the suburbs where I "laundered" $1,000,000.00 dollars a month for various businessmen. Because I was taking it to another level, I needed to insulate myself from detection. I had the brilliant idea, bribe as many Internal Affairs detectives and other high ranking officials as possible. And a soon as an outside law enforcement official made an inquiry about me, I would be two steps ahead of them; it worked like a charm. By the time the F.B.I., D.E.A. or P.P.D. left the Internal Affairs building, somebody was at my house. The money had them hooked liked a research monkey. There were more loyal to me than their wives.

As time moved on, I developed what's called a "swag." Regular cops ate at McDonalds or brown bagged their meals; I ate at Bookbinders. Regular cops purchased their clothes from Burlington Coat Factory; I brought my clothes from Versace. Regular cops wore $35.00 loafers; I wore $2,000.00 Alligators. Regular cops brought $10.00 to work; I brought $10,000.00. Cops drove Ford Tauruses. I drove an S-600's Mercedes and an 850 C.I. BMW. My pride was at an all time high, and I began to have a disdain for blue collar workers. It was like they were fools. I developed a saying *Gangsters do what they want to do and suckers do what they are told to do!*

As time passed, I began to experience paranoia and unrest in my soul, **because I knew at some point this lifestyle had to come to an end, and I knew the end would be costly.** I would ride down the street in the police cars and see a siren come on and would subconsciously pull over. You may laugh hysterically at this but as shameful as it sounds, it was true. Whenever the officers would congregate at an event, I would often withdraw. Other officers could pet the K-9 dogs; whenever they saw me they barked out of control. My logic was they were the only ones in the department who knew who I truly was.

As Paranoia set in, I needed time to think because my behavior was getting out of control. I had the perfect idea. Every year I would go out I.O.D. (injured on duty) at least three times a year; all my injuries were faked. I once walked by a trash fire in Suburban Station. As I approached, I contacted police radio to send me a medic unit because I had smoke inhalation. I actually spent so much time off the job that the rookies and cadets thought I was a new recruit when I returned to work. Clearly my behavior demonstrated that I was screaming out for something – but never knew it was for God!

One day, I went to my mom's house to check on some money that I stashed there. As I began to walk up the steps, I saw my sister Pam and greeted her. Pam is a tall, beautiful lanky, brown skinned woman that I characterized as peculiar, as she believed in Jesus Christ. She said to me, "Boy, when are you going to give your life to Christ?" I responded, 'Christ is cool, I believe in Him, but I believe all religions lead to God.' My mother butted in and said, "Boy, I told God several years ago that if He gave me a male child that I would give it back to him. When are you going to change?" I responded, 'Momma, I'm cool. I feed the homeless and help old people. I'm alright!'

When I left the house, I saw something on my 850 C.I. B.M.W - it was that mysterious looking branch. I sat there for ten minutes and began to ponder the conversation I had with my mom and sister, and when I walked toward the branch it mysteriously blew away.

Four months had passed by, and I received a tip about a federal organization inquiring about me and another coming to kick my door down August 15, 1994. That news had me rattled and deeply concerned. I sent my wife and kids over to my wife's mother's house and cleaned my house from top to bottom. The day when the raid was executed I intentionally left the door unlocked and the

A.T.F. stormed into my residence hoping to find me and a cache of AK-47's, MAC II's, and Tech-9's. When they left, the search warrant read, "Confiscated pictures of Mr. McLaurin, his children, and his Blue Cross/Blue Shield card."

Because the cat was almost out the bag, I began falsely seeking God. I began reading the Bible, praying that this thing would pass me, and eventually it did. The A.T.F. talked to at least 200 people, but couldn't seem to build a case on me. As soon as the heat was off, I ditched the Bible and began to "pop my collar." I thought that I had beaten the Fed's and my pride was at an all time high. I graduated from Philly blue collar crimes and took my show on the road. I started doing business with the Italian Mafia, and it wasn't the Philly mob, I went straight to New York. I didn't stay at that level long before I was dealing with one of the most sophisticated, most violent mobs known to mankind - the Russian Mafia. Both organizations loved my style. I was smooth as butter. Couldn't catch me on the phone, couldn't hear me on a wire, couldn't catch me on a video, and I was 6'6" and 330 pounds.

As I began to climb the mountain of success in my organization, I became very reckless. I began picking up my paycheck from my job once a year, while the average cop was waiting by the door every Friday. My chief became very frustrated. He knew he had a dirty cop on his hand, but he couldn't prove it and the more I became aware of that, the more arrogant I became.

One day I made the biggest mistake I ever made in my life. I came within inches of blaspheming Almighty God. One night while out with my crew en route to our hangout at a club called *Studio 37*, we pulled up in an entourage of fancy cars, people started yelling, "Big Mont! Big Mont!" My bodyguard said to me, "Wow captain, these people think you are God!" I responded 'If I'm not God, then I'm the next best thing!'

As I attempted to enter the club, a short elderly woman walked through the crowd to give me a Christian tract. I looked at her and said, "Thanks ma'am," and reached into my pocket to pull out $20.00. She said "No thanks son. God don't want your money, he wants your soul." She gave me one of the spookiest stares, smiled and walked away.

As I walked into the club, I walked in a trance. I couldn't get the lady off my mind and I told my bodyguard to catch a ride with one of the crew, I needed to go home. On the way home I stopped to get some gas and after I pumped the gas I sat in my car pondering what the lady said. I then pulled the tract out my pocket and read a biblical scripture from Jeremiah1:5 and 1:12. The first scripture read, "Before I formed you in your mother's womb I knew you." The second scripture read, "I watch over my word to perform it." All I could think about was what my mom and sister said; "Boy when are you going to find God?"

Two months went by and I began to ponder heavily on questions like who is God? What is His name? Why are there so many religions?

One day, I made a power move and earned $75K from it. I went to a restaurant to pickup my share from a devout Muslim brother. As we broken down the proceeds and talked about the crime, he began to say, "Inshallah, Inshallah, Inshallah!" In Arabic that means, "If God is willing." As I exited the meeting, I slipped into a deep trance and said 'What does God have to do with robberies, guns, extortion and the like?' I pulled up to my house to check on my children, while en route to my secret stash house. On my way to my stash house, I began to talk to God and this was the exact conversation:

'God who are you, are you the God of the Muslims, Christians, Catholics, Jews Hindus, Buddhist, Jehovah Witnesses? Who are you?' It was a Thursday evening in the month of July approximately 8:30pm. While sitting at the red light, my car shut off. I put my hazards, on and began to mumble some expletives. I got out of my car lifted the hood. It was so clean and technologically sound that it was almost impossible to think that something could be wrong with the car, a brand spanking new 850 C.I. that the Philadelphia 76ers forward Stackhouse had bid on but I beat him to the punch.

I got back into the vehicle to call A.A.A. The sky darkened, leaves and wind started blowing and my head tilted towards the heavens. I physically heard a voice say, "This year I am going to show you My face!" The thing was so powerful, I urinated on myself. The elements began immediately to clear up. I turned the key once and the car started right up. I pulled over to a side street called Mansfield. I sat in the car looking like Buckwheat from the Little Rascals, eyes large like a deer caught in headlights and lips looking like I ate a bag of flour. I got out the car and paced back and forth. While pacing an elderly Caucasian woman approached me and said, "Son, are you O.K.?" I responded 'Yes ma-am' as I looked at her strangely. I paced again thinking about the voice, turned around and the old lady was gone. I began to question myself, 'Wait a minute. I don't smoke, don't drink. What in the hell is going on here? What are these strange occurrences?'

I returned to my car, made a u-turn and went back home in a trance. As I pulled into the garage my wife said to me, "What's wrong with you? Something has scared the pure bleep out of you!" I ignored her, walked into the house tracking mud on the carpet with my boots on. My wife began frantically screaming at me as I ascended the stairs to my bedroom. I got in bed fully dressed lying on my back, with my boots on thinking about the host of strange events. Morning came and I hadn't slept a wink. I called out from my job and took my car to the dealership. As I began to tell the dealer the story, he looked at me and said that it was mechanically impossible for this type of car to stall. This car could run underwater for half an hour and not cut off. That's when I knew God was calling me. The Bible states "pride goes before a fall." In order for God to reveal himself to me my pride had to be broken; and boy did he pick a "pride breaker!"

Two months had passed by and my wife and I had a two-week separation. During that time, I had sex with a friend of mine who knew all of my intimate secrets. At that time I thought it was the worst mistake of my life as she had become pregnant. Not only was she pregnant, she became obsessed with breaking up my marriage and destroying my life. She set no limits pursuing this endeavor.

One night while at work my wife called, and I knew something was wrong. When I answered the phone she said "Hey daddy?" I responded, 'Yes.' She asked was it true I was having a baby…Mother (bleep). My friend Sal told me I passed out. **That's when the "party" really got started.** This female went to my wife's job showing her stomach, to my daughter's school showing her stomach. She showed up at my wife's hair salon and needless to say, my wife didn't handle it well; she was headed for a nervous breakdown and she persecuted me every day all day. It was like a living hell from the time I opened my eyes until I slept.

Four months into this young lady's pregnancy she began to have complications and it was rumored that she lost the baby. My wife began to regain her sanity. And again, I ditched my Bible and started popping my collar. I stepped up my game and moved to hijacking truck loads of computers, electronics, etc. When the major crimes task force became aware, I met with a technological genius that put a chip in my police scanner that allowed me to hear their every move. If they surveyed in Philly, I would be in New Jersey; when they moved to the left, I moved to the right.

At some point, I became utterly disillusioned. One evening while on duty on my lunch break I was sitting on the 11th floor at the Marriott Hotel at a swanky restaurant. I ordered an $800 meal for myself and my partner, and I ordered a $700 bottle of wine. I then pulled out an authentic Cuban cigar (which was illegal) and began looking down at the police officers running to and from my police headquarters, which was adjacent to the restaurant. As I began to stare I said in my heart *Look at these fools and suckers*.

Four months passed by. I was at my mom's house playing football with my nephews and my son. My mom hollered out the window, "Son, come here quickly!" I didn't know what was wrong, but I knew it was serious as I ascended the steps. She said, "Son sit down." I said, 'What mom, what? Come on what's wrong? She said, "That girl had the baby. It's an eight pound baby boy named Jeremiah Lamont. I sat down on my mom's bed and said, 'Oh my God!' On the way home I could not stop staring at my son in my car because I knew that this news was going to separate me from the one thing I cherished most in my life - my wife and children.

One month passed and my wife was driving past my mom's house and the young lady was sitting on my mom's porch with the baby. All hell broke loose in my life. I began to look for God again. I began to attempt to heal my wife with my money and gifts but it wasn't working. I then planned on leaving the state, but I had one more move to make. I couldn't run away from my problems long enough to restore sanity in my life.

Four days after my son's birth my mentor and father figure Jeremiah Shabazz died. I was lost. I had no real male figure to turn to. It couldn't have happened at a worse time. The preceding day before Jeremiah died, he called me to bring him some underwear. When I arrived his body was sort of lifeless and he spoke in twenty minute intervals. He began to point to a Bible which was autographed to himself and asked me to read the 23rd Psalm to him. That sort of blew me away because I knew that Jeremiah was Muslim. What really puzzled me is how Psalms 23 starts off with *The Lord is my shepherd*,' but in John 10 Jesus says that He is *The Good Shepherd*. I scratched my head and pondered heavily about God while I continued to stress out about losing my family and planning my next big move.

Six weeks passed by. While planning my next big score, a score came to me. The captain in the Russian mob asked me to facilitate him off duty police officers to repossess stolen jewelry; in actuality it was to be a home invasion of two wealthy Russian spies. I agreed. What I didn't know was at the times I spoke to Igor, phone taps and surveillance cameras were rolling; I had run into an investigation. The FBI from the Southern District of New York came to Philadelphia to investigate me; they heard that I was a police officer, so investigations intensified. They met with the chief of my department, and he led them to the ATF. After meeting with the ATF, the Southern District of New York was convinced that they had a full-fledged dirty cop on their hands.

During the months of March and May the plot was being planned and implemented. On May 5, 1998, the plot went down, at approximately 8:15 AM. Although the FBI knew it was going down they didn't know the exact location due to the cryptic conversations that Igor and I we're having.

That morning while walking through the subway, I ran into my ex-girlfriend's mother, Louise Burbage. She had been ministering to me about Jesus for five years. I walked up to her, hugged her and said, 'Hey mom.' she said, "Don't hey mom me. That thing you got yourself into is going to literally kill you." I asked her what she was talking about. She said "You will see, you will see." I thought to myself how in the hell does she know about this thing? Did I have a billboard on my head that said I was committing crimes?
Moments later, my team called in and said that they were safe and it went down. But some things were required of them that were not in the script. I told them to call me as soon as they got back from New York, and we would meet.

While waiting on the two soldiers to come back from New York, the Russians were calling in discussing the home invasion and the tapes were rolling. The Russians phones were wire, but our phones were not. The soldiers came back and reported that they executed the job with precision, but it wasn't what they agreed to. I asked, 'Where's the money?' They said, "The Russians have it." I called Igor and said, 'Hey Gary, how are you? How did things go?' He responded, "They went okay. I'll see you in Philly in about three hours." I responded, 'Okay good. Do you have my birthday present?' He said, "Sort of." Until today I don't know why I said that stupid statement. The F.B.I. picked up the call.

Three hours passed by. I met with Gary, and he was short $50K. I was visibly upset and told him that he would have to "have mine or be mine;" a term meaning get my money or pay the consequences. Igor related my statement to his boss Alexander Spitchenko, a serial killer and boss of the Russian mob. He replied, "Give us a couple of months." While awaiting a response from the Russians, the FBI convened a task force to follow me; the ones who surveyed the Russians after the May 5th job. I kept a very low profile. I pondered why I made that bonehead statement *You got my birthday present?* and how it could affect the state of my family.

Two months passed by and God was about to show me His face. One night while getting ready for work I put on a t-shirt full of holes. My wife said, "Lamont, take that t-shirt off. With as many t-shirts you have in your drawer, why would you wear that holey t-shirt?" I turned around and replied, 'Because I am a holy man. My wife replied, "Imagine that!"

That night, while working a twelve hour shift, I received a strange radio transmission:

"Radio to 189."

'189, Proceed'

"Report to 1234 Market Street, ninth floor."

There was something eerie about this call. I began to think, okay *what I have done recently?* I had taken a few trucks. I then called my hijackers to see if they were in custody. They both picked up when I called. I'm thinking, thinking, thinking. I got my head together and proceeded to 1234 Market Street to my department's floor.

My chief greeted me as I came off the left elevator. He said "Good morning Lamont." I thought to myself *What is my worst enemy greeting me good morning? Something is desperately wrong."* He then offered me a seat. "Can I have your gun belt?" I took a sigh of relief and said to myself, *He didn't take my badge, so I'm cool.* I had been brought up on charges at least ten times, and every time I won; and in my mind, this was my eleventh victory.

Boy did he pull the wool over my eyes. He said, "Sit tight Lamont. Would you like coffee?" I declined. Then he shouted out, "Clear!" That day, my life changed forever. I saw a procession of FBI agents come down the corridor, and it appeared that they wouldn't stop coming.

"Good morning Mr. Lamont. My name is Agent Bosch. I am from the Eurasian Task Force and we have a criminal complaint alleging that you are an enforcer for the Brigade. (Otherwise known as the Russian Mafia) All your co-defendants are arrested, and you are looking at thirty years jail time!"

I dropped my head down and said 'Oh my God.' My chief began to rip my Police shirt off as if it were a trophy; and then the games began.

While being escorted out of the building, I observed a huge crowd (some hecklers, some haters and some sympathizers.) What was telling was when I looked up, I looked at the Marriot where I had been eating when I made the statement *Look at these suckers.* At that point I would have given my left arm to become a sucker.

The FBI took me down to the federal building to interrogate me. When I wouldn't cooperate, they took me to Lewisburg (United States Penitentiary) where the motto is *"Only a killa get a pilla!"* I didn't stay at Lewisburg long before I was transferred to Salem County Correctional Facility in New Jersey. There I made my first phone call. My wife was devastated. Around 9:30 PM, I stood in my cell by a window and said 'Lord God, you have revealed yourself to me several times and I ignored you. Just do me one favor? Just take care of my family. It doesn't matter what happens to me.' Three days passed by.

I began asking other inmates about the possibility of bail. They all responded "Big man, it don't look good! The Feds have a 98% conviction rating."

July 21, 1998, I was transported to Philadelphia to have a bail hearing at the federal courthouse. My family hired a famed beast of an attorney, Dennis Cogan. While in custody, he paid me a visit. He said, "Lamont from what I have read in the criminal complaint, I believe we have a good chance at trial! But Judge Melison is a redneck that wouldn't give his grandmother bail for jaywalking!" I went back to my cell and began praying: *To the god of Islam, Buddhism, Jehovah Witness, Catholic, Hindu etc. Whoever you are, I need to see my children one last time. If you are God show me your face and tell me your name.*

While praying, I could hear the judge slamming his gavel down screaming, "No bail!" One half hour later they called me.

When I walked into the court room dressed in an orange jumpsuit, I saw I had about 400 supporters. My family was in the back praying in what Christians call "tongues." My wife had congestive heart failure and passed out in the court room. As I approached the defendant's stand, I motioned to the crowd of onlookers – the big thumbs down sign! My sister Marilyn shouted, "The blood of Jesus! You're coming home today!" I said to myself, *Just what I need, a bunch of religious clowns.*

While sitting at the defense table an old vision came to me. I began thinking about the time I fell off the cliff. I looked up at my sisters praying for God to save me. I glanced back and then I saw the same vision, just 30 years apart.

Prior to the start of my hearing, I heard voices whispering, "Hey Lamont, Hey Lamont!" I turned around to see where the voices had come from. It was the two ATF Agents, Wesco and Siwicki, whom searched my house and conducted subsequent investigations. I turned around quickly to compose myself, because I nearly lost my bowels.

Moments later, prior to the start of the "fireworks," the judge emerged from his chambers. When Dennis Cogan mentioned that he was a redneck, I thought he meant it metaphorically; this judge really had a neck that was beet red! My eleven codefendants were denied bail. The Assistant US Attorney said he was saving me, the best for last!

Then the AUSA began his opening statement. The court observed that he removed his tie as he spoke these words: "Your honor, I present you Lamont McLaurin; an angel by day, the son of Lucifer by night. Mr. McLaurin is not only a sinister predator, but working in the capacity of a police officer makes him diabolical. I would give you the eleven Russians back as trade for one Mr. Lamont McLaurin." The AUSA closed and my attorney spoke for two minutes followed by a closing statement. The judge said that he needed to take a recess, and that court was adjourned five minutes. The AUSA was visibly upset, but he held his peace until the verdict.

As court resumed, the judge re-emerged from chambers with a strange look on his face. I looked back at my family and gave them the big thumbs down. My sister stood on her feet and said, "The blood prevails."

The judge then ordered me to stand up and rendered a decision and prophecy to me simultaneously. These were his exact words (and there are a cloud of witnesses today to confirm my story):

"Mr. McLaurin, you are a relatively young man, thirty-five years old, with a very bright future. I spoke to your sister Sarah Derious and she assured the court that if given bail, you would adhere to the conditions."

In a sudden rage, the AUSA jumped out of his chair exhibiting a tantrum! He actually tried arguing with the judge that my indictment came from the White House; if I remained in jail chances would be better for the government to squeeze valuable information from me. The judge gave the AUSA a strong admonition and threatened to have him held in contempt. The judge then resumed speaking.

"Mr. McLaurin, what do you have for bail?"

My sister spoke out "$450,000, Your Honor."

The judge replied, "The court will accept your offer." My lawyer and I stood in utter disbelief. The attendants in the court room applauded the judge. The marshals escorted me to my cell. All my codefendants were in utter disbelief about the judges ruling.

On the way back to Salem County, I really scratched my head. What in the hell happened in that court room?

Two days passed and my sisters came to get me from jail. Upon my release my heart was beating a mile a minute because I wanted to know exactly what my sister said to the judge to cause him to give me bail.

My sisters arrived, and as we traveled down Market Street en route to 76 West, I asked my sister Sarah (who's nicknamed Renée) 'Where did you meet that judge?'

She said, "I never met the judge a day in my life!" You could have bowled me over with a bag of cotton balls! **Remember, in front of at least 400 onlookers that judge stated that he talked with my sister.** Then I really began to ponder.

When we pulled onto my block, the neighbors looked at me as if I were a leper. Children that usually played in my yard were told not to go to my house. My heart was broken because I love children; they are my passion. I shook it off.

I began to plan my legal defense. I sold all my cars for pennies because of the costs for my legal defense, Dennis Cogan is one of the only lawyers that win against the Feds. I began calling in cash from several police officers who owed me money I loaned them for mortgage foreclosures, car repos etc., and all totaling $60,000. One guy responded, "Call the fire department because you just got burned." Another one said "Meet me at police headquarters at 8:01 PM," knowing that I was on house arrest and couldn't come out after 8 PM.

As tribulation mounted up, I gravitated towards God. On April 21, 1999, I went to church to get some peace and comfort, but did so covertly because the general consensus was that I was Muslim and most of my crew was Muslim; and the man who raised me was Muslim.

When I arrived, I sat in the back row hoping that nobody would call on me for a testimony or a comment. As the message concluded, my hopes were dashed as a preacher (prophetess) named Roxanne Darden called me out; these were her exact words (I wrote them down):

"The man in the dark blue suit..." I turned around to see if someone else had on a dark blue suit. She then said "Could you stand please?"

"God told me that you are looking at a huge amount of time in jail. You are in travail over it, but you won't see a fraction of what's predicted." I see large numbers like 70 or 80 years."

After she finished speaking I said to myself, *Yeah, this is some church gimmick,* because what I was facing was at the most 30 years if convicted.

When God had decided to break my pride, He didn't use a hammer. He used a jackhammer! Since I had lost my job at Transit Police, a friend of mine hired me at his medical center picking up clients for $250.00 per week. I picked my check up on time! The car I drove was now a 1989 Ford Aerostar that my enemies called my "stretch Navigator." I was monetarily broke. My crew had run for the hills and when I called, there was no answer. All I had was my family and God.

Four months passed by and I received a telephone call from my attorney. He said "Hi Buddy, I need for you to brace yourself. The ATF is going to indict you tomorrow and they are going to kill you in the media. They are estimating 70 to 80 years if convicted."

I pondered how I was going to keep this from my wife and children. That morning I was arraigned and indicted at the federal courthouse. My wife called and said, "Lamont, what are we going to do? I can't take this anymore. I didn't sign up for this."

I then reflected on what Prophetess Roxanne Darden said to me and how accurate her prophecy was four months prior to this indictment.

That second wave of tribulation blew over and just when I thought it was safe, the unthinkable happened. Yep, my wife popped her collar. I began noticing changes in her schedule. On my birthday, she told me she was going to the supermarket and didn't return for a week. When she came back, the first thing she did was ask me to run her some bath water. As I came at her to choke the life out of her she said, "I wish you would." If you look at me wrong I will let the cat out of the bag and you know exactly what I'm talking about!" She stopped me dead in my tracks because she had a secret that could literally turn my lights out.

Over the next few months, my wife was having it her way. She became bolder and bolder by the day with a new lover; she had *no stops and all goes!* She would pull in front of the door with the guy, kissing in front of me, knowing that I couldn't come outside and that she was still holding a major secret.

This thing began to agitate me. I called the guy and told him he could have my wife, but if he showed up on my block again he would have a big problem. Because he was soft and had an idea of whom I was, he stayed away for a week or so. As time moved on, he became bolder. I had a plan, and the perfect person to put my plan together. My team ran for the hills, but you always have one or two special friends that ride till the end. I met with two of them separately, putting together a contract murder on my wife's friend. The person that would carry this out was blood thirsty and had a reputation for his craft.

One cold December night the plan went into action. While waiting for the gunshot blast and my wife's screaming that her friend's brains were all over the car, I sat waiting in my room in the dark. A mysterious voice came to me and said, "Lamont, this is going to end your life. Call this thing off; its coming back to blow up in your face!" I immediately got on my 2-way Nextel and hollered, "Slides Up, break out, keep it pushing!" That meant, "Police are present, don't come back." I heard the screeching of tires as the assailant pulled off – I pondered whether the voice I heard was my conscience speaking or God; time would tell!

As days went by, so did my pride. Now when I drove down the street, people who used to hail me wagged their heads at me. My popularity was virtually nonexistent. My money had dried up; I had become a "regular Joe" in a matter of months. *God didn't forget me though. He put angels around me because with what I was about to face I was going to need them.*

The heat was eventually on. The Feds allowed the ATF to get the first shot at me and boy did they have a pre-show and after party with me! The Daily News read, "Trouble Is Piling Up For Lamont McLaurin!" And Fox News correspondent, Dave Schratwieser did an exclusive "…Russian mafia featuring Lamont McLaurin." The phone rang again and again with family and associates giving their condolences, because I was a dead man walking.

Two days before the trial my attorney called me with a message from the Feds: "Take a plea or take a knee"- as if to say "If you take us to trial and lose, we are going to hit you so hard you will be on your knees crying out to God." I couldn't take a plea because it would involve the two guys I sent to New York and I would never want to place them in my shoes. Ten days passed by and their prophecy came true... guilty on all counts. The Daily News headline read "McLaurin Faces 88 Years," and as I cooked dinner for my son and daughter that evening, I did just that; fell to my knees.

A month went by. It was now the day I faced sentencing with one of the worst judges in the Eastern District of Pennsylvania, Judge Eduardo Robreno. I had come to the point where I had no more emotions left, no fear, nor sorrow. Right before Judge Robreno imposed the sentence he said, "Mr. McLaurin, when is your trial in the Southern District of New York?" He asked that question to see if I was cooperating in the case. If I would have said, 'Judge my attorney and I are seeking to resolve the case.' he would have taken it easy on me. But I said, 'Your Honor, the fireworks started on September 13.' He then turned my lights out with the maximum.

As I stood motionless, something very shocking happened. Instead of the judge revoking my bail and sending me straight to jail, he gave me sixty days to surrender.

When I arrived back home my ex-wife was astonished. She thought that they would keep me. I observed that she had all of my things packed to go to my mom's, because life with her had come to a tragic end. Two weeks went by, and I hired the best appeal attorneys on the planet, Fred and Cheryl Sturm. They took a serious interest in my case as well as my plight. Seven weeks passed by. I began seeking God, going to church and reading the Bible. Again it was a fake look, not as fake as the last, but still not fervent.

Two days before I had to report to jail, I met with my pastor. I thanked her for all her support and the mentor she placed in my life, Ernie Chandler, an angelic host in human form. She explained to me that I wasn't going to jail on that date and time. I snickered saying to myself, *Having faith is one thing, being crazy is another. If the judge said report in, you better report in!*

My ex-wife gave me a "going away party" the day before I was to turn myself in. Some of my friends from the Nation of Islam came and offered encouragement; God personally sent them because I was going through it. Before I went to bed, I called my pastor to say my last goodbyes or sort of tell her thanks for her encouragement. She said "Hey man what do you have planned for tomorrow?" I responded 'Nothing much just turning myself in at 10:00 AM at Farrington FCI.' Then she said, "What is it going to take for you to believe the word of God? I said, 'I know, but it is what it is! This is the real world I'm going to jail tomorrow.'

The next day was also my wedding anniversary. That morning, at 8:15 AM I called my pastor to "put egg on her face." I said, 'Look, thanks for everything, God is still good but I have to go.' She replied "O yea of little faith!" I then said (to myself), 'She may need to see a psychologist!'

The phone beeped. I clicked over to the other line and it was my attorney in the U.S. Marshal's office stating the third circuit court of appeals gave me an extension because the case may be overthrown. I hung up the phone and looked at my wife. She said, "What's wrong, what's wrong?" I said, 'I can't believe it, I can't believe it. That was just the my attorney saying that I don't have to go to jail!'

This news disappointed my wife, because she was ready to close the chapter on me to start a new life with her new boyfriend. I ascended the steps like Moses at the end of the Ten Commandments in awe and shocked that prophecy was fulfilled. My sister had predicted it, and it had happened!

A few days went by and I attended Bible study with Pastor Ernie Chandler. Ernie was a great teacher. He was patient, kind, and scholarly. But, what he didn't know was he had a wolf in the sheepfold. At Bible study I used to fantasize about the different women I used to fornicate with and the one I was going to fornicate with as soon as I left Bible study. Although Ernie was a great teacher, the Word was not alive in my spirit. Reading the Bible was like being in chemistry class; when Ernie prophesied to me he gave me great comfort because he led me to believe that God blessed sin.

A month passed and the case was reversed. The Assistant US Attorney spoke with the judge in the Third Circuit and related to the judge how important it was that I be put in jail, not because I was planning more crimes but the Justice Department in Washington was calling for my head. Two weeks passed, and my wife began picking up the pace of disrespecting me by having her significant other, which called for me to move to my mother's house - two weeks before my self surrender.

On June 7, 2000, God showed me his face through tribulation. I went to kiss my mom goodbye. I went into the next room and witnessed my sons Lamont, Jeremiah and my nephews all linked together in the same bed. I had never in my life experienced so many emotions at one time. I cried in my heart as I descended the steps. One of my mentors and good friend Steve Rocher (who worked for Transit Police) drove from Philadelphia to Elkton, Ohio - a six hour ride. Steve said I slept the entire way, depressed. I arrived at Elkton, Ohio FCI where a guard said, "We were waiting for you!"

As I became acclimated with my new environment the pain of leaving my loved ones bothered me. I called my wife and her boyfriend picked up the phone. He taunted me with questions like "Who is this?" and saying "Your wife is in the shower! Nice bed you have Lamont," knowing I was powerless and had to grin and bear it. I bit through my lip thinking of how many ways that I wanted to punish this guy.

A few weeks went by, and I hooked up with some Philly dudes that I knew. We played ball, lifted weights, ate together and I started to calm down.

Right when my sanity seemed restored, I heard over the loudspeaker "McLaurin pack out." Pack out was a term that meant you're going to another jail but you don't know which one. I packed my stuff and boarded a bus en route to the airport, shackled from head to toe. Like in the movie, Conair I boarded a plane that had at least 50 marshals surrounding it. The airplane sounded like a car that needed a tune up.

Most inmates on the plane were high-profile, so I guess I fit right in. While in transit I struck a conversation with a serial killer, and I explained my case to him. He then informed me I had been appointed for diesel therapy. I asked what was that? He responded, "Your ID number ends in 748. You are from Philadelphia; the crime happened in New York. Your ID should be 053, 054. 748 is a Washington number so since you are going to trial, they are attempting to break you before you go. You may not get off and re-board this plane for another six months!"

Wow! His prophecy came true! Over the next six months I was dropped off to, at least twelve penitentiaries, placed in special housing units, and couldn't make phone calls, get mail or get visits. I was finally placed at Metropolitan Correctional Center, Manhattan, New York. I was in a hallway unit for two days, and then in a cell flooded with water. There I met a gentleman named Ali Mohammed. He was Bin Laden's right-hand man in the Tanzania bombing. Seated across from me was 'Sammy the Bull Gravano,' the ex-underboss turned informant of the Gambino family and famed gangster "Pistol Pete" from the "Sex Money Murder" gang in New York City. It was definitely a culture shock; 23 hours locked in a cell the size of an apartment bathroom, that was flooded and rat infested with a cellmate that smelled like an auto shop at all times!

I slept twenty hours a day for the next two weeks, depressed and stressed out. One day, something woke me up and said, *Read the Bible*. I then summoned a guard named Arnie, and asked him for a Bible. He looked at me if to say "You weren't reading the Bible out there, why are you reading it now?" He gave me a Bible and that's when my strength and hope came back to me. God mingled a spirit throughout the unit. He put a guy next to me named Andre Dula Martin from the "Sex, Money Murder" gang; he had me laughing just about all day. I also had a theological study with the Arabs from Al Qaeda, daily and the more I read the Quran, it built my faith in Jesus. I observed that Mohammed prayed for sin in Surat 5:29 and Suart 4055. But Jesus forgave sin in Mark 2:5. The Koran also mentioned Jesus name 99 times and Muhammed only 25 times. It referred to Jesus as Messiah, Word of God, and also the Spirit of God.

Then one morning while I was doing push-ups in the dark, I glanced over at the Egyptian clerk during one of my breaks. I could see him but he couldn't see me. I was in utter shock as he motioned as if he was performing the sign of the crucifix near his heart. Because I couldn't believe what I saw I began to watch him covertly every morning. I saw this three more times that week.

While in theology study, I began to concentrate on the Egyptian cleric. He knew the Koran backwards and forwards and also knew the Holy Bible. One day while going to the recreation roof. I was alone with the Egyptian cleric. The three men from Al Qaeda had a court hearing. We walked around and around the rooftop. I kept thinking how I would ask this man if he was Christian and why he made the sign of the crucifix instead of praying like normal Muslims. All of a sudden my questions flooded from mouth; he looked at me as if he could kill me. His eyes opened wide and his hands trembled. He responded in a stern voice, "Why do you ask? Who told you that?" I responded 'No one, I just observe you making the sign of the cross in the morning.' He stared at me with a blank stare and said, "What I am about to tell you could get me killed. Yes I am a Christian. If anyone knows, I am a dead man here and most certainly in Egypt." I stayed in my cell for the next few days, because this revelation had me troubled. I couldn't believe what I was experiencing and I had to digest it all.

Three weeks went by, and we were in the flow studying. While the three Arabs were prepped to go to court, an officer was caught off guard, not following the procedures of the special housing unit by handcuffing the inmates before they came out their cells. Because of this major error, he met his fate with a plastic shank in his head area - that penetrated through his brain and protruded out of his eye. The Arabs began shouting "Allah uh Akbar, Allah uh Akbar" which means "God is the greatest." Backup arrived in seconds because this incident caught on camera. When the C.O's arrived, they beat the Muslims unmercifully.

Because of the incident, two days later the Muslims and I were separated. I went to general population, and they stayed in the special housing unit. There I experienced culture shock all over again. I was now in Seven North, a 100 man unit. The unit was suffering; the men's souls were literally dead, they became victim of the federal government; they never knew, it was even a shock to most foreigners.

The federal prison system may be the cruelest oppressor on the earth from a judicial perspective. I met a gentleman that the Bureau of Prisons denied diabetic medication. He went blind. When he went to court, his lawyer told the judge that he had congestive heart failure, high blood pressure, kidney failure and that the bureau blinded him. The judge added five years to his 10 year sentence. I met another young man Daniel Egipicia. While working his full-time job, a government informant solicited him to help him rob a drug dealer. He agreed and he walked to the location but changed his mind. He was arrested and sentenced to 25 years just for saying yes.

As time went by, my faith became stronger in the God of the Bible. I no longer believed every wind of doctrine. I developed conviction. I began a Bible Study with some Spanish gentleman and it began to blossom. Soon, every nationality was in the church worshiping God. One day, I was asked to sing with the choir and lead a song entitled "Lord Prepare Me to be a Sanctuary. As the choir began to sing the spirit began to move. I put my head down began to laugh. The choir stopped and sternly asked what was so funny. I replied, 'Nothing, nothing.' What I was really laughing at was my attire; a bright orange jumper and a pair of $1.50 skippers, for I remember the time my bodyguard said, "Hey man these people think that you are God, and my response "If I'm not God, I'm the next best thing!"

Time moved forward to my second trial, just around the corner. God surrounded me with angels in human form. These were not the people who I previously gave money to. They were people that I never paid any attention to that had no obvious motives. God placed them in my atmosphere to hold me up when I was ready to let go. A month before trial I received devastating news that my attorney Dennis Cogan had to pull out of the case. The trial was a multi-codefendant case that was scheduled to last six months; I only had enough finances for one month. I didn't sweat it much because I wasn't in New York on that day. The victims didn't know me neither did the person testifying against me, so in essence it was a meatball.

Two months had passed and the fireworks began. What I thought was a meatball turned out to be a meatloaf. They put the brakes on me with that one silly statement, *Do you have my birthday present?*

As I sat in the Marshall's office, so they could process my second conviction, one of the marshals shouted across the room, "Hey Jim, what is today's date?" Jim replied "December 14." (That is the day of my first son's birthday.)

When I arrived back at the unit, I waited in line for the phone to speak to my son. When I finally got a chance to call, his mother's boyfriend picked up the phone and said, "Hey loser, I guess it's all downhill now?" (Once again I imagined the torture I could inflict upon him if the opportunity arose.) My wife answered the phone and said, "It's all over the news, how could you do this to us?" I responded 'You didn't say that when the bread was coming in!' she stated "Yep, the bread stopped and so did your communication…say hello to your son for the very last time!" My son answered the phone with a quivering voice. "Daddy when are you coming home?" I couldn't muster up the strength to respond or even say happy birthday. I slowly hung up the phone and let out a cry for God that literally shook the building.

I began to lean on God because of the pain. The devil began to work on my mind. He began to tell me that Elder Chandler was a false prophet and Dr. Miles was false also, because they both promised me victory with my criminal trials. Satan began to say that prophecy from Pastor Roxanne Darden was a hoax, crapshoot, a good guess and that every encounter that I had with God - from being held up by the branch on the cliff to the three fish caught on one hook was an absolute coincidence, fabrication, and delusion.

On the other hand, I kept hearing God say "Remember, remember, remember…" On December 24, 2000 at 1:00 AM, I was in my cell laying on my back gazing at the stars in the sky and the atmosphere. It was a cold, beautiful and brisk night. After two hours of star gazing, I recapped my life and my situation. I spoke to God, 'God if you are still with me give me a sign. Allow one of the stars to blink or something.' Ten seconds later this one particular star gave off a miraculously bright light. I stared until the sky went back to normal. I got up out of bed and told myself, *You are going crazy!* I immediately returned to my bed and gazed at the sky for 50 to 60 minutes then I spoke to the Lord again. 'Look God, I am not saying that I don't believe you but I wanted to make sure that this wasn't a coincidence. If you do it one more time I will believe you forever.' Twenty seconds later I saw the same star with the same strange light in the same area of the sky. This time I didn't move. I was right where God wanted me to be to believe him for every day.

As time went forward so did my troubles but God had given me a strange peace throughout it all. My feelings and emotions for my wife began to change; the hurt and anger began to dissipate. When I first came to the penitentiary, I received at least 15 to 20 pieces of mail a day; it reduced to one or two pieces and then eventually none. It was all good because when my so-called friends failed me, I began to press into God.

Two months passed by, and I was indigent. I needed to pay for a new appeal attorney. I called my wife to get the bail money. She seemed to be a bit more cordial, but at this point she still was not to be trusted. I gave her all of my info and she swore to retrieve the money and give half to my sister. We agreed she would keep half. Every week for two months I called my sister. I would ask, 'Hey, did your wife give you the bail money?' and she would say, "Lamont, you will never see that they have money, because she spent it!" I replied 'She would never stoop that low.' I started calling her and she gave me a different story each week. Week one, the bail people said they have to get the okay from the feds. Week two, they said two more weeks. Week three, they put the money in my account and my creditors took it. I responded, 'I was born at night not last night enjoy the money.'

I called back a week later, and the phone number was changed; she really cut me off! I was troubled but God put me in perfect peace. I prayed for God to put a mentor in my son's life after months of not talking to him.

One day around 2:00 PM, I was praying for a phone call or letter from my son. At 4:30 PM during mail call, I received a big orange envelope with a picture of my son's new mentor and basketball team. His mentor was a young man named Paul Gripper, whom I taught how to make his first dollar, although it was illegal money. He felt indebted to me, because I taught his first real hustle.

Things began to prosper for me; no more hurt nor pain. My young son, Jeremiah, moved with my mom and I knew he was safe because he was the apple of her eye. That was a two-fold blessing, because he gave my mother a reason to live. My daughter Lauren went into the Navy.

As I began to trust God with my stuff, he began to trust me with his stuff. I built a ministry that brought life to the jail. Not only did God teach me His Word, but he gave me the uncanny ability to counsel men and to perform miracles through the legal system by teaching me criminal law.

When I slept in the morning, men would congregate outside of my cell anticipating my awakening. Men that were looking at 60 years of jail time had sentences reduced to 3 to 5 years. (*see But By My Spirit). Men that were contemplating suicide began to encourage others. I had correctional officers coming to me for marital counseling and while their marriages were being healed, officers' wives would reciprocate by cooking me meals. The CO's were serving me home cooked meals in my cell! God had placed so much favor on me that all men would call me blessed. I had two ministries, one in the day and one at night. The daytime ministry's work was for the souls who had come to an end of themselves. The night ministry was for demons only; this was also for men whose indictments said they were serial killers, etc., who were too proud to be associated with God in public.

As time passed, I felt like I wasn't in jail. If someone asked me to leave, I would have actually contemplated it. I had federal judges writing me letters as if I was a lawyer. The Justice Department wrote me a letter on how I revolutionized a prison and gave me a sizeable check. God had given me so much favor that each day in prison seemed more like 12 hour days. I was so busy that I couldn't feel the sting of depression, loneliness, and suffering of jail. Actually these were some of the better times of my life.

One night while things were quiet and all the inmates were locked in their cells, I began to ponder the statement I made to my wife when I put on that holey t-shirt (and unwittingly prophesied to myself that I was a holy man).

One morning, I was laying on my cot staring at the World Trade Center on September 11, 2001 at approximately 8:20 AM when my next door cellmate José Indio Mendoza knocked on the wall and said:

"Hey Biggs you up?"

I responded, 'Yeah I'm up. You Cool?'

He responded, "Yeah I'm cool but I have a really strange feeling that something big is going to happen today!"

I responded, 'Like what? A riot or something?'

He said, "No Biggs, something major, something like catastrophic."
I said, 'Really? Like what?'

He said, "I don't know Biggs but it's scary!"

I then asked, 'What are you reading this morning?'

He said, "Matthew 24 in the New Testament."

I said, 'For real? I'm on the same chapter.'

Our conversation ended for approximately eleven minutes. Then we witnessed the first plane hit the World Trade Center. We seemed so close we could just reach out and touch the building. It was a sound so loud and devastating and surreal that words, television or video cannot adequately describe what actually happened; you had to experience it for yourself.

Indio Jumped up screaming "I told you so, I told you so Biggs, I knew something was going to happen!" Moments later we put down our Bibles and turned on the radio to 1010 Wins A.M. As we listened and watched the sky, the second plane hit and New York fell to her knees. As news spread that a second plane hit, I began to hear the chants from the Umar (Muslim brotherhood). "Allah uh Akbar, Allah Uh Akbar…" which means "God is the greatest." It was only the Arab Muslims from Turkey, Iran, Saudi Arabia, and Iraqis who where chanting, not the African-American or Hispanic American Muslims. It was almost as if they knew something.

All of a sudden, the entire prison was locked down because Abdul Rahman was in the prison, the orchestrator of the first World Trade Center attack. The belief was that the prison was next. As the calamity unfolded, it appeared that Armageddon was here. As we looked out the window men and women from all walks of life were calling out to God. People were running frantically as if 400 foot tidal waves were pursuing them. Limbs were hanging off their bodies and asbestos was covering their faces. You had Sikhs, Muslims, and Jews - every religion crying out "God help us!" or "Jesus help us!"

A police station was directly across the street from the prison. I looked out at the police on their knees praying. This was much too much excitement for me to experience. I searched the Bible for prophecies; I found at least ten connected to the World Trade Center. None floored me more than Matthew 24:29: *In that day the sun will be darkened and the moon will not give her light."* Jesus spoke that 2000 years ago. I looked out the window in 2001, and exactly what he had spoken 2000 years ago, I was looking at it with the naked eye. In New York on that day, the smoke darkened the sun and at night the smoke was so dense that the moon would not give her light. We were twisted like door knobs.

A year passed. America was at war on two fronts. I began writing my judge about my sentencing with negative results. One day, I phoned home and my bodyguard told me that everybody was getting locked up and the Feds were tearing the city up investigating my third racketeering case. My initial response was trepidation, but by this time I was used to it. One morning I got a knock on my door and the C.O. (Correctional Officer) said:

"McLaurin, court!"

I responded, 'Wrong person, I don't have a sentencing date.'

The C.O. said, "Just get ready, we are taking you down!"

I got prepared, but instead of taking me to the original court, they took me to a place called the "Old Court" where secret cooperation agreements transpired.

Upon arrival at the court the C.O. handed me over to the marshals and the marshals handed me over to the Feds. My attorney was late getting there so we just sat looking at one another. My attorney arrived 15 minutes later, and then the fireworks began.

The FBI revealed the racketeering case and that out of 50 people, 49 people were cooperating. The case was open and shut. Just about everything I thought I got away with 10 years ago was relived that day as if I just did it. As I listened intently, I said to myself, *I am finished.* Then they told me about four homicides that I was directly connected to and I knew they were somewhat on the wrong track because the details were way off. But when they mentioned that attempted contract murder on my wife's friend Rodney, I knew they were on point.

They offered me a chance of a lifetime - to be taken out of jail and go back to Philly the same day if I gave names, details, and so on. I respectfully declined the offer and told them that I would not be going to trial on this case. The Philadelphia agents left and promised to be back with an indictment. (When the Feds promise you an indictment, you usually get it!) The marshals escorted me back to the C.O.s, and they escorted me back to my unit. I became very withdrawn the next couple of days, because I wondered about the case, God's promises and my future.

One Sunday, I was watching a football game. During half-time, the NFL channel did an interview on the New England Patriots linebacker, Willie McGinest. During that interview, I marveled at how he had a successful career, gave his mother everything she wanted and had a nice well-rounded family; everything he talked about, I dreamed about. As I sat there, I questioned God about my condition. I first said, 'God why me? Why couldn't it be me retiring from the NFL with a nice family, money, etc.?' I then became angry with God over the choices that I made.

All of a sudden the Spirit of God probed me and began to reason with me.

The Spirit said, "Lamont who did you think gave you your police officer career?"

I said, 'You (God).'

The Spirit then said, "Why did you thank me?"

I said, 'Because I knew it was you not me.'

The Spirit said "Okay then how did you get in here?"

I said, 'My choices.'

The Spirit then said, "Okay now we can talk. Have you ever played sports?"

I answered 'Yes.'

The spirit asked, "What sports did you play?"

I answered, 'Football, wrestling and boxing.'

The Spirit then said, "Where you average, above-average or great at any of the sports?"

I responded, 'Above average.'

The spirit said, "What in life where you absolutely great at that men recognize as great?"

I thought about five minutes and said, 'Theology.'

The spirit said "Correct!" He then said, "How many times have you been indicted?"

I replied, 'Three times.'

He asked, "Where they all federal?"

I replied, 'Yes.'

What types of oppressors are the Feds?

I replied, 'The worst!'

He replied, "What's the likelihood of a police officer receiving three separate indictments in a period of two years for three separate crimes, research it and see what you come up with!"

Then I sat in a whirlwind. The Spirit spoke and said, "Lamont if the first indictment didn't hit you the second indictment would have! If the second didn't hit you, then the third would have! You had no way of escape; it was predestined. The devil put the evil thought in your head years ago… *If you can't beat them, join them.* You then controlled men's minds through organized crime. What the devil didn't know was that you were in training to bring men into my kingdom!"

The conversation stopped for one half hour.

Then I heard a voice from heaven say "I am going to show you great and mighty things that you do not know."

I went to Jeremiah 33:3, there were the exact words staring me square in the face. I began to say, 'That wasn't God; I was tripping or was it?'

Later that day I went to Bible study. The topic of subject was Jeremiah 33. The next day at church, I sat back preparing to hear the Word of God. A beast of a preacher Rev. Winston Kato said, "Turn to Jeremiah 33:3." I sat back, closed my eyes and chuckled. The Reverend nicely stopped the service and asked, "Lamont is something wrong?"

I responded, 'No, I'm sorry, it's just something personal.'

Nine more months passed by, and I received the dreaded knock. "McLaurin, court!" My stomach was in knots as I prepared to face the inevitable. As I sat in the holding cell, I reflected on Jeremiah 33:3. Four hours later, the marshals led me to the courthouse where the Feds were waiting with smiles. They said "Hello Mr. McLaurin." I responded to the greeting.

My lawyer and I began a private meeting. I asked, 'What's up?' She said, "I don't know but we are here to listen... more than likely they have you." Later, the case agents laid out their case; the information they didn't get from me, they got from my old associates in graphic detail. I knew I had to take a plea, but for how much time?

The Feds offered me an open unprecedented plea that would allow this judge who I had favor with to sentence me.

The judge asked the case agents, "What took this case so long?"

They said, "They changed AUSA's prosecutors nine times and it ran into a statute of limitations issue." I almost literally passed out. It is unprecedented for the government to change prosecutors over three times. With this case it was nine. If God wasn't looking out for me, then who was? Although the statute of limitations ran out, I could have fought the issue. Wisdom said let sleeping dogs lie because I had some stuff that I didn't want to be uncovered.

Six months had passed to the day; it was time to meet the judge. My best friend, Sam Anderson and Kim Ferrell were in the back of the court room praying their hearts out. There was a strange light in the court room; the Spirit of God was on me and they could see it.

The AUSA customarily painted me as a mixture of Adolph Hitler and Stalin. My attorney then said a few words, but nothing touched the judge like the repentance letter that I wrote a month prior to my sentencing. She sentenced me to 36 months and as I was leaving the courtroom she uttered these words, "Mr. McLaurin, I believe in you." Until this day whenever I get a moment I reflect on those words and my strength is renewed.

It was a somber moment when I got back to the unit because my fellow inmates knew their comforter (not that I am associating myself with the Holy Spirit) was departing. Two weeks later, I was notified to "pack out" and the unit threw a going away party for me. It was one of the saddest days of my life, so I thought. The following morning made the preceding night look like a New Year's party.

As I began packing my property men, from all walks of life were crying out, "We are going to miss you Biggs." Mexican, Dominican, Russians, Italians, Jamaicans, Japanese and Chinese. The closer I got to the door, the louder it became. As I descended on the elevator, each floor was screaming the same thing. I boarded the marshal's van. The C.O. said, "Wow, I have been doing this for 20 years and I've never seen anything like this. Those men thought you were **God**." I thought of the time my bodyguard said the exact same thing years before.

I arrived at a new prison and was greeted by some familiar faces. I observed big money criminals from oil companies like Enron, major exporters, embezzlers etc., whose names I'd rather keep anonymous. I built close relationships with them. I meditated on the revelation that God had given me. It persuaded me that God set me up to be rich.

As time progressed I begin to receive a litany of mail, almost every month, with tragic news of someone diagnosed with kidney failure, cancer, congestive heart failure and the like. In the next wave of mail came the obituaries. I questioned salvation and after studying the Bible for all it's worth. As narrow-minded and intolerant as it appears, it's just an inescapable fact that if a person's sins are not ATONED for, they can never see life again. Unfortunately, all my friends that perished were unsaved.

Sometime in August 2005, I received the worst news of all. I called my bodyguard named Marlowe "House" Medley, and he told me that he was diagnosed with congestive heart failure. When he gave me the news, I immediately talked to him about salvation. He switched the subject and started talking about the Philadelphia Eagles and how he didn't believe in the Bible or a historical Jesus; he believed in evolution and whatever happens just happens. I was quite disturbed about his thinking because "House" was not just a friend; he jumped in front of bullets to save my life on several occasions. Additionally, he supported me financially while I was incarcerated and looked out for my children. I went into a prayer and told God that I didn't want to go to heaven without him.

On October 16, 2007 at 10:45 AM I was released from physical custody; a free man! My dear friend Sam, nicknamed "Old Faithful" and his wife Stacy picked me up. On the ride back home my mind raced a thousand miles a minute. I meditated on the very day I left home and the pain I felt descending the stairs. When I arrived home it seemed that God set the stage in reverse. He actually turned all my pain into joy. I sat on the steps looking at my sons and my nephews. They were all at least six feet tall, healthy and of a sound mind. It's like I never missed a beat. Everyone was there except my daughter, she was overseas in the Navy.

Two days passed, and I went to see my bodyguard. He was very excited to see me and I made sure I didn't talk about Jesus. As we rehashed old times and played PlayStation, I began to silently pray for his soul and spirit. God confirmed to me that he wrote his name in the Book of life.

As time moved on, I thought about the prophecy in Jeremiah 33:3 and how God was going to fulfill it. I reached out to certain friends of mine that were in the industry and precious metals. As I began attempting to consummate deals the monetary aspects were astounding. I became somewhat disillusioned about the prophecy of Jeremiah 33:3 and actually communicated with real-life millionaires and billionaires. As time passed year after year, I would get close to closing a deal and then the rug would be pulled from underneath me. It was very frustrating because I was still serving God, but at the same time I was attempting to fulfill my vision or chase a dream.

As time moved forward, I landed a job at a school. I started out in maintenance and in time was promoted to history teacher and then Department Head of Theology. I began to prosper in everything, in every area of my life - spiritually, socially, financially and the like.

In 2008, I wrote my first book entitled *If God Doesn't Permit a Woman to Preach Then God Must be a Sexist.* Sales went well and are prospering as we speak. I said to myself "Is this is what God meant in Jeremiah 33:3." Nevertheless I still had a void in my life that was unsettling.

My bodyguard "Big House" was not well. Days would pass by and I would find out that he passed out at the mall, he passed out at the wheel of his car, on the street or he's was at Temple Hospital, Chestnut Hill Hospital or Mercy Fitzgerald. One night, he shared with my son Lamont and I that the doctors said he had less than a year to live. It was a very somber moment because the real question was not the fact that he was going to die, but where was he going when he died. What if the Bible is true? I began to discuss salvation with him… he put his hand up as if to say pause.

One day in the month of June, "House" called me and said "I have something to tell you that you wouldn't believe in a million years!" I thought it was some news about one of our friends dying, jailed or news about the Philadelphia Eagles. It was none of the above. He told me that he received Christ as his Savior and Lord, and he wanted me to be at his baptism at Enon Tabernacle Baptist Church on June 25, 2012. I looked up into the sky and fell backwards on my bed.

On June 25, 2012, I attended the baptism, and it wasn't your average baptism! It was a "state of the art" baptism. On an HD (high definition) screen, I saw House submerged into the water and when he emerged, it seem like another person emerged. As the on lookers cheered a stranger out of nowhere came up to me, shook my hand and said, "God will do great and mighty things that you do not know."
God had fulfilled his promise. On May 5th of this year, I was over Marlowe's house. After some time as I was exiting I said 'Well you won't be going back and forth to the hospital this year because the Eagles have Chip Kelly a high octane coach!' (He seemed to always go to the hospital when the Eagles lost.) He responded, "Yeah your right," Chip Kelly or no Chip Kelly, I am finished with this hospital thing."

On May 10, 2013, my best friend and bodyguard went to be with the Lord. God watched over His word and performed it.

God is a God that is attracted to storms. God lives in the realm of the impossible. When modern science says "Impossible," God says, "Possible!" When the doctor from Harvard says your family member or yourself has six months, God says I will add 35 years. When the foreclosure sale says date certain, God says pause. When the job says "Pink Slip," God says, "Promotion!"

In my experience, it seems as though God always meets you in those hard places, those desert wilderness places, where people either cannot help you or will turn their backs on you. I thank God today that when I was faced with the impossible. He made all things possible. When people turned their backs, He was still riding to bring me to an expected end.

While closing out this manuscript I was watching one of my favorite detective stories Criminal Minds. As the agents identified the suspects, this question came to mind: "What is his end game? The term " end game" essentially means *what is your ostensible purpose and what do you hope to accomplish*. As I pondered the question, I came across several conceivable probabilities. Was it for money? No, because the book is monetarily accounted for. Was it for fame? No. My past is very shameful; I don't want to parade it around. Was it to debate and belittle other religions and make myself look like a spiritual giant? No. I think offending other religions or what people freely choose to believe is evil.

So what is my end game, as the author of this book?

After careful consideration, I believe with all my heart that I wrote this manuscript in light of a secular term that I coined when I was in the business of organize crime, and that is, "When I eat… my crew eats, which means I want for my brother what I want for myself.

Approximately 37 years, I went hungry and looked everywhere to get something to eat. I stopped at the church, and I saw bipolar members say one thing do another and scamming preachers (send me $300 and I will send you a magic handkerchief as point of contact and God will answer all your prayers.) I stopped by the mosque, but I just didn't feel God's presence there. I stopped by the club wearing $10,000 outfits and went home feeling empty. I tried making money legally and illegally but still felt empty. I tried "playing the shots" (tricking with different women) and still felt empty. But on July 9, 1998 at 10:00 AM in the morning the worst day of my life, became the best time for my life. The most fearful time of my life turned into the boldest time of my life. After 37 years of starvation and wondering who is God, which religion is the right religion, does God answers prayers, what is my purpose, how do I find God, and most of all how can I find this peace and joy that I looked everywhere for, I have finally found it.

Today, I know clearly who God is and I am convicted by my belief. Today I know what my purpose is in life and the reason I was born. Today, I have peace and joy whether I have $10,000 in the bank or $10 in my pocket. Today, I do not need a person of the opposite sex to make me feel complete. Today, I know when I die where I am going and the certainty of my return. Today, I don't see myself as other people see me but only as God sees me. Today I can say with certainty to the dialysis patient **God is all you need!** Today I can say to the cancer patient that **God is all you need!**

Today, I can say to inmates doing life that **God is all you need!** Today, I can say to the disgraced official that God is all you need! Today I can say to the AIDS carrier that God is all you need!. Today I can say to the drug addict that there is no high like The Most HIGH and **God is all you need!**

Today after 37 years of starvation, I can say with all manner of confidence that I found the very bread of life. After plodding through all of life's ups and downs, victories and losses in every human there is a need, and the best advice I can give you is after you have experienced with every idea and piece of advice that comes to mind be sure of this one thing; **YOU WILL NEVER KNOW GOD IS ALL YOU NEED UNTIL YOU REALIZE GOD IS ALL YOU HAVE.**

Dinner has been served. Bon appétit!!!

You'll Never Know God Is All You Need Until You Realize God is All You Have

www.LamontMcLaurin.com

www.ingramcontent.com/pod-product-compliance
Lightning Source LLC
Chambersburg PA
CBHW060514100426
42743CB00009B/1307